access to history

HENRY VIII *and the* REFORMATION *in* ENGLAND

Second Edition

access to history

HENRY VIII *and the* REFORMATION *in* ENGLAND

Second Edition

Keith Randell

Hodder & Stoughton

A MEMBER OF THE HODDER HEADLINE GROUP

Acknowledgements

The front cover shows Henry VIII by Joos van Cleve, reproduced courtesy of The Royal Collection.

The publishers would like to thank the following individuals, institutions and companies for permission to reproduce copyright illustrations in this book:
Henry Nelson O'Neil,'The Trial of Catherine of Aragon' Birmingham Museums and Art Gallery, page 27; 'The Allegory of the Reformation' from *Book of Martyrs* by John Foxe, The Royal Collection copyright 2000 Her Majesty Queen Elizabeth II, page 45; 'Sir Thomas More' by Hans Holbein the Younger © The Frick Collection, New York, page 55; The Royal Collection copyright 2000 Her Majesty Queen Elizabeth II, pages 105 and 106.

Every effort has been made to trace and acknowledge ownership of copyright. The publishers will be glad to make suitable arrangements with any copyright holders whom it has not been possible to contact.

Orders: please contact Bookpoint Ltd, 130 Milton Park, Abingdon, Oxon OX14 4SB. Telephone: (44) 01235 827720. Fax: (44) 01235 400454. Lines are open from 9.00–6.00, Monday to Saturday, with a 24 hour message answering service. Email address: orders@bookpoint.co.uk

British Library Cataloguing in Publication Data
A catalogue record for this title is available from The British Library

ISBN 0 340 78215 3

First published 1993
Impression number 10 9 8 7 6 5 4 3 2
Year   2005 2004 2003 2002

Copyright © 1993, 2001 Keith Randell

Typeset by Fakenham Photosetting Ltd, Fakenham, Norfolk.
Printed in Great Britain for Hodder & Stoughton Educational, a division of Hodder Headline Plc, 338 Euston Road, London NW1 3BH by The Bath Press, Bath.

Contents

Preface

To the general reader

Although the *Access to History* series has been designed with the needs of students studying the subject at higher examination levels very much in mind, it also has a great deal to offer the general reader. The main body of the text (i.e. ignoring the 'Study Guides' at the ends of chapters) forms a readable and yet stimulating survey of a coherent topic as studied by historians. However, each author's aim has not merely been to provide a clear explanation of what happened in the past (to interest and inform): it has also been assumed that most readers wish to be stimulated into thinking further about the topic and to form opinions of their own about the significance of the events that are described and discussed (to be challenged). Thus, although no prior knowledge of the topic is expected on the reader's part, she or he is treated as an intelligent and thinking person throughout. The author tends to share ideas and possibilities with the reader, rather than passing on numbers of so-called 'historical truths'.

To the student reader

Although advantage has been taken of the publication of a second edition to ensure the results of recent research are reflected in the text, the main alteration from the first edition is the inclusion of new features, and the modification of existing ones, aimed at assisting you in your study of the topic at AS level, A level and Higher. Two features are designed to assist you during your first reading of a chapter. The *Points to Consider* section following each chapter title is intended to focus your attention on the main theme(s) of the chapter, and the issues box following most section headings alerts you to the question or questions to be dealt with in the section. The *Working on . . .* section at the end of each chapter suggests ways of gaining maximum benefit from the chapter.

There are many ways in which the series can be used by students studying History at a higher level. It will, therefore, be worthwhile thinking about your own study strategy before you start your work on this book. Obviously, your strategy will vary depending on the aim you have in mind, and the time for study that is available to you.

If, for example, you want to acquire a general overview of the topic in the shortest possible time, the following approach will probably be the most effective:

1. Read Chapter 1. As you do so, keep in mind the issues raised in the *Points to Consider* section.

2. Read the *Points to Consider* section at the beginning of Chapter 2 and decide whether it is necessary for you to read this chapter.
3. If it is, read the chapter, stopping at each heading or sub-heading to note down the main points that have been made. Often, the best way of doing this is to answer the question(s) posed in the Issues boxes.
4. Repeat stage 2 (and stage 3 where appropriate) for all the other chapters.

If, however, your aim is to gain a thorough grasp of the topic, taking however much time is necessary to do so, you may benefit from carrying out the same procedure with each chapter, as follows:

1. Try to read the chapter in one sitting. As you do this, bear in mind any advice given in the *Points to Consider* section.
2. Study the flow diagram at the end of the chapter, ensuring that you understand the general 'shape' of what you have just read.
3. Read the *Working on ...* section and decide what further work you need to do on the chapter. In particularly important sections of the book, this is likely to involve reading the chapter a second time and stopping at each heading and sub-heading to think about (and probably to write a summary of) what you have just read.
4. Attempt the *Source-based questions* section. It will sometimes be sufficient to think through your answers, but additional understanding will often be gained by forcing yourself to write them down.

When you have finished the main chapters of the book, study the 'Further Reading' section and decide what additional reading (if any) you will do on the topic.

This book has been designed to help make your studies both enjoyable and successful. If you can think of ways in which this could have been done more effectively, please contact us. In the meantime, we hope that you will gain greatly from your study of History.

Keith Randell

1

Introduction: Henry VIII and the Reformation in England

POINTS TO CONSIDER

As you read this chapter for the first time make a conscious effort to identify the different ways in which historians have studied the Reformation in England. If you don't know how you will be studying it, now is the time to find out.

A large majority of those living in the United Kingdom of Great Britain and Northern Ireland in the early 21st century play virtually no part in organised religion. They seem to feel that it is not important, that it is not relevant to their lives. This has not always been the case. For more than 400 years, from the 1530s to well within the lifetimes of many people still alive today, the tensions between various groups of Christians were a very real part of national life. Those living in Northern Ireland will well understand how significant, even destructive, the dislike and distrust between Catholics and Protestants can be. On many occasions over the centuries similarly dramatic situations have arisen in England, Scotland and Wales because of tensions between these two Christian traditions. This book explores the events which eventually led, in England and Wales, to a previously united Church splitting up.

This religious divide began during the reign of Henry VIII, and was completed while his children occupied the throne, in what has traditionally been called the English Reformation. As a result of the English Reformation, Protestantism became the country's official religion, the Church of England, headed by the monarch, became its established Church, and adherents of the 'old faith' (Catholicism, headed by the Pope in Rome) found themselves variously ostracised, persecuted or relegated to second-class citizens as the prevailing circumstances dictated.

1 Approaches to Studying the English Reformation

KEY ISSUES What are the main features of the approaches typified by Froude, Dickens and Haigh? Which approach is currently most in favour?

For centuries the overwhelming majority of historians accepted uncritically that their task was to recount the doings of the rich and famous. This meant that political history dominated and that women (unless the absence of male heirs forced them into the spotlight) were rarely mentioned. 'Ordinary' people provided the backcloth, especially in times of war or civil disturbance, but were treated much like the extras in a Hollywood film – they were seen but not heard. It is therefore not surprising that most histories of the English Reformation have concentrated on the actions of kings and queens and of those close to them. This 'top-down' approach rapidly became established as the norm during the early decades of History's existence as a respectable academic discipline. One of the most prominent English historians of the nineteenth century, J.A. Froude, completed his 12-volume history of the mid-Tudor period in 1870. The analysis he developed provided a framework of study for several generations to come. The terms 'official Reformation' and 'political Reformation' were used to describe what was thought to be of real importance in England's change from Catholicism to Protestantism. The story was thought of as having a prologue and four main chapters. The prologue was Henry VIII's struggle to persuade the Pope to grant him a divorce from his first wife, Catherine of Aragon. This took place between 1527 and 1533. Each of the 'chapters' covered the events of one monarch's reign. In the first 'chapter', (1533–47), Henry VIII took over the Pope's powers and much of the Church's property, while generally succeeding in preventing change in the Church's teachings or practices. He established an independent Church of England that was Catholic in doctrine. His son, Edward VI, was an ardent Protestant and, although he was only a child during his six-year reign, he actively supported those who ruled in his name when they introduced radical religious beliefs and practices. By the time he died in 1553 England had become a Protestant country. Henry VIII's elder daughter, Mary, was queen from 1553 to 1558. She was a Catholic who tried to reverse what her father and brother had done. She was succeeded by her younger sister, Elizabeth I, who was a Protestant. Because she reigned for 45 years, (1558–1603), she was able to ensure that the Church of England moved permanently away from Catholicism. In all four parts of the story the doings and beliefs of the population at large were mentioned only in passing.

However, from the time of Froude onwards, the 'top-down' school of historians explicitly recognised that there was a second strand – the 'popular Reformation' – to the story, but they were certain that it was of less importance than the 'official Reformation'. This view was effectively challenged for the first time by A.G. Dickens who published his masterly *The English Reformation* in 1964. This book did much to establish a new orthodoxy. It was based on the contention that a 'bottom-up' approach, concentrating on the activities and enthusiasms of ordinary people, would provide a more meaningful explanation of how England became Protestant than would an account of the 'official' or 'political' Reformation. But Dickens did not suggest that the actions of government were unimportant. He merely argued for a shift of emphasis in favour of the 'popular' Reformation. He wrote his book according to the new balance he advocated. In order to do this he had had to carry out an enormous amount of original research into topics (such as the spread of Protestant and the demise of Catholic beliefs and practices among the general population) that had previously been largely ignored by historians. In the process, he had uncovered numerous new sources of evidence and had developed new techniques for evaluating them. At the same time others were arguing that the English Reformation ought to be thought of in different conceptual terms.

The Reformation in England had traditionally been thought of as an 'event'. It had been portrayed as a long drawn-out event, lasting for up to 70 years (1533–1603), although with the major actions all falling within the first half of the period. The problem was that it had been assumed the individual happenings that comprised it were all linked together in a chain of cause and effect, giving unity and coherence to England's change from being a Catholic to being a Protestant country. As a result, the readers of narratives of this 'event' could hardly avoid reaching the conclusion that the outcome of the story had been inevitable from the outset. This was especially so as the majority of both authors and their readers regarded the Reformation story as an account of the triumph of good over evil and therefore as 'progress' and something to be welcomed. Unease about these unstated assumptions grew in the decades after 1920 when objectivity (as opposed, in Reformation studies, to a commitment to either a Catholic or a Protestant point of view) became the hallmark of academic respectability and when historians became more aware of the dangers of hindsight. Some of them recognised that the accepted ways of looking at the English Reformation were good examples of flawed thinking – of knowing what occurred in the end, and of viewing previous happenings primarily as steps towards that final position. It seemed to them that the end-point had been reached as much by chance as by design and that the direction of events could have been altered by random factors at almost any time. They, therefore, came to the conclusion that the coherence given to the 'event' by most historians only existed in the minds of later observers and certainly had not been apparent at the time. In the light of this fact, they judged that it might be more accurate to think of the English Reformation as a 'process', (a sequence of related rather than closely linked happenings), and not as an 'event'. This change in perception made particular sense when adopting a 'bottom-up' approach to what happened. Dickens's way of looking at things especially lent itself to this concept, and his book was effectively a charting of the 'process' by which Protestantism replaced Catholicism in England. For some time historians acted as if the concepts of 'event' and 'process' were incompatible, and that one must be 'right' and the other 'wrong'. However, it is now accepted that, as long as the dangers of assuming cause and effect and of using hindsight are kept in mind, both concepts are helpful in gaining an understanding of what the Reformation was, what were its causes and what were its effects.

Although Dickens has remained the standard text on the English Reformation, and is likely to be so for some time to come as a result of a substantially re-written second edition of the book being published in 1989, the central conclusion he reached (rather than the approach he adopted) has been disputed by a numerous band of 'revisionist' historians. Dickens argued that Henry VIII was able to carry out his political Reformation – breaking with Rome, establishing himself as the Supreme Head of the Church in England, and dissolving the monasteries – largely because his actions coincided with both the advanced stages of a decline in popular support for the Catholic Church and a rapid spread of Protestant beliefs. His contention was that the Reformation from below happened early and speedily. The 'revisionists' have generally maintained the exact opposite. Basing their conclusions mainly on a sequence of detailed local studies, they have advanced the view that Protestantism was adopted by most of the people of England and Wales towards the end of the Reformation period (if at all) – 'late and slowly' as opposed to 'early and rapidly'. Indeed, they have produced telling evidence to support the argument that Catholicism stubbornly remained the majority belief in some parts of the country throughout the Tudor period despite all the efforts of central government and the missionary activities of Protestant preachers. But the 'revisionists' have not yet been able to win for their interpretation the status of being the new orthodoxy. Much of the evidence they have used to support their views is too partial and too open to differing interpretations to allow them to establish a totally convincing case. However, the balance of opinion is certainly tipping in their favour. This is because many historians have been convinced by the interpretations put forward by Christopher Haigh, the best-known of the 'revisionists'. In particular, there has been considerable support for his contention that there was not just one English Reformation. He argues that there were several 'political' Reformations between 1533 and 1559. He claims that they should be treated as distinct happenings and that it is unhelpful to think of them as chapters in a single event. His view is that the English Reformations were separate but linked.

2 The Reign of Henry VIII

> **KEY ISSUES** What approaches could be used when studying religion during the reign of Henry VIII? Which approach is this book going to follow?

Historians used to be in no doubt that the years 1533–47 were a vital part of the English Reformation. The supporters of the traditional 'top-down' approach viewed the break with Rome and the establishment of the Royal Supremacy as the secure foundations upon which the Church of England was built, while those who followed Dickens in pressing for much more attention to be paid to the activities of the people at large and who accepted his general chronology for the spread of Protestantism were equally convinced that the die was cast before Henry was in his grave. For all these people it made sense to talk of the 'Henrician Reformation' as being an event and/or a process of considerable historical significance.

Starting in the 1970s and gathering pace in the 1980s a sequence of research articles and academic books was published that threw considerable doubt on the prevailing orthodoxies. It was suggested that at a macro-political level (the actions of the king and of parliament) nothing was done before 1547 that was both important to the Reformation and difficult to reverse. The significance of the break with Rome and of the royal supremacy were unchallenged, but attention was drawn to the fact that it was an accepted part of the constitution that whatever one parliament passed a later one could rescind. This was proved by the way in which the parliaments of Mary's reign restored the link with Rome, revoked the royal supremacy, and reversed the Protestant doctrinal changes that had occurred while Edward VI had been king. It was accepted that the dissolution of the monasteries was effectively irreversible once most of their former lands had been sold to the aristocracy and the gentry, but it was argued that the closure of the religious houses had been peripheral to the real Reformation – that the dissolution could have taken place without there being a Reformation and that there could have been a Reformation without the monasteries being dissolved. On the micro-religious level (the beliefs and practices of ordinary people) enough examples of change being minimal or non-existent were uncovered to allow it to be argued that the evidence presented by Dickens was untypical and that the majority of people were untouched by Protestantism before the second half of the century. The cumulative effect of these 'revisionist' historians' findings was to open a new debate – a debate that has, as yet, not been concluded.

In the process those historians who are more interested in Henry VIII than in the Reformation have been reinforced in their belief that, when studying the whole of the period 1509 to 1547, it makes more sense to think of religion as an aspect of politics rather than as a topic in its own right, forming the first act of a four-part saga of England's change from Catholicism to Protestantism. Thus, for them the 'top-down' approach continues not only to be acceptable but also to be necessary if a meaningful account of what happened is to be constructed. *Henry VIII and the Reformation in England* has been written very much from this point of view. It is to be thought of as the second half of a two-part attempt to explore the important aspects of the politics of Henry's reign – the first part being *Henry VIII and the Government of England* in this series. The book should be of interest to those whose prime objective is to gain an understanding of the Reformation, but it is likely to be especially helpful to those whose focus of study is Henry VIII, the man and the monarch. The structure of the chapters that follow is dictated by the way in which the early Reformation is normally discussed, but it is hoped that a clearly identifiable underlying theme is provided by a consideration of Henry VIII's actions and what his motives for them were.

Throughout this book it is assumed that you have already studied the issues and events covered in *Henry VIII and the Government of England*. It might be helpful to refresh your memory about this material before proceeding further.

Summary Diagram
Introduction

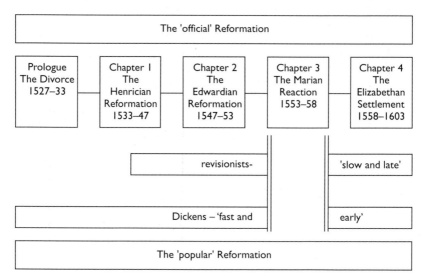

'top-down' historians

The 'official' Reformation

Prologue The Divorce 1527–33	Chapter 1 The Henrician Reformation 1533–47	Chapter 2 The Edwardian Reformation 1547–53	Chapter 3 The Marian Reaction 1553–58	Chapter 4 The Elizabethan Settlement 1558–1603

revisionists-	'slow and late'

Dickens – 'fast and	early'

The 'popular' Reformation

'bottom-up' historians

Working on Chapter 1

Before beginning to read the next chapter it would be a good idea to stop and make conscious decisions about what you hope to gain from this book.

If your aim is to acquire an understanding of the first stage of the English Reformation, the most effective strategy to follow is clear. First of all re-read this introductory chapter. As you do so ensure that you understand i) the traditional 'top-down' approach of studying the Reformation as a coherent event, ii) the 'bottom-up' emphasis that was argued for by Dickens, iii) the 'early and rapidly' interpretation that led Dickens to view Henry VIII's reign as playing a vital part in the English Reformation, and iv) the reasons why 'revisionist' historians doubt whether the years before 1547 played a significant part in England's change from being a Catholic to being a Protestant country. Then read chapters 2, 3, 4 and 5 in turn. It would not be a good idea to miss out any of them. After reading each chapter make certain that you understand the main sequence of events described in it. For some people this will best be done by checking through the list of Key Dates at the start of each chapter. Then ask yourself the question, 'What part did the events described in this chapter play in turning England into a Protestant country?'. If your initial answer is 'none', stop to check that you have considered 'indirect' as well as 'direct' causes. Finally, read chapter 6 and act as far as you think appropriate on the advice given in the study guide.

However, if your hope is to deepen your understanding of Henry VIII and the politics of his reign, your study strategy will need to be different. It will not be surprising if you have come to the conclusions that reading this chapter has not helped you greatly and that you do not want to spend further time on it. But you will find that chapters 2, 3, 4 and 5 have been written with your requirements very much in mind. You will probably already have formed tentative conclusions about Henry VIII as a king and as a person. If you have, you could use this book to test out, refine and add to your existing opinions. One effective way of doing this would be to head separate sheets of paper with the adjectives (sometimes a related group on a single sheet) that you think best describe him. Then, as you finish reading about each of his actions, assign it to one or more of your sheets. When you have finished the book examine your sheets carefully. What conclusions could be drawn about sheets that have had nothing added to them? What do you do if some of your new sheets have headings that contradict old ones?

2 The Divorce

POINTS TO CONSIDER

As you read this chapter for the first time, try to do two things. Make a mental note of the order in which events occurred between 1527 and 1533, and start to form an opinion about why each of the main characters involved acted as he/she did.

KEY DATES

1527		probable date of Henry's decision to divorce Catherine of Aragon
1528–29		failed attempt to obtain a divorce using Cardinal Campeggio
1529	Oct	Cardinal Wolsey removed from power
1532		Thomas Cranmer appointed Archbishop of Canterbury
1533	Jan	secret marriage of Henry and Anne Boleyn
	Mar	Act in Restraint of Appeals
	May	declaration that Henry and Catherine of Aragon had never been married because the papal dispensation allowing it had been invalid. Henry's marriage to Anne Boleyn declared legal

During the first three-quarters of the twentieth century generations of British school children were taught that the Reformation in England took place largely because Henry VIII wished to obtain a divorce from his first wife (Catherine of Aragon) so that he could marry his second (Anne Boleyn). The 'historical truth' that students learnt was that Henry fell uncontrollably in love with Anne Boleyn soon after he learnt that Catherine of Aragon would no longer be able to bear him children, and would therefore not be able to provide him with the son he so fervently desired. Because Anne Boleyn refused to accept the king's sexual advances until they were married, which drove him almost to distraction, and because Henry was astute enough to recognise that, in any case, a son born to Anne out of wedlock would at best have a contested claim to succeed him, divorce became an urgent necessity. But only the Pope could dissolve marriages and he remained stubbornly unwilling to do so in Henry and Catherine's case, despite years of threats and browbeating from England. In the end the only way in which Henry could get what he wanted was to take over the Pope's powers within his own kingdom and arrange the divorce for himself. This he did and the Reformation took place (in essence the establishment of an independent Church of England) as an unintended side effect of political and personal necessity.

Surprisingly enough, the 'top-down' school of historians (notably Professor Scarisbrick) have reached somewhat similar conclusions after carrying out exhaustive research of the type that was beyond the scope of their nineteenth-century predecessors who had established the schoolbook orthodoxy. Naturally there have been significant refinements and changes of emphasis made to the old orthodoxy, but in its essentials it has remained intact. In particular, the central idea continues to be that the engine driving England towards its Reformation was political rather than religious.

1 Beginnings

> **KEY ISSUES** When did Henry decide to seek a divorce from Catherine of Aragon? Why did he decide to do this? Why did he think the divorce would be achieved easily?

Despite the efforts of many researchers, it has proved impossible to locate reliable evidence about the timing of Henry's decision to attempt to bring his marriage to Catherine of Aragon to an end. It must now be accepted that the best historians can aspire to is to identify the period (rather than the exact date) that is the most likely one, given the circumstantial evidence that exists. It is probable that the king made up his mind later than has often been suggested. Rumours that Henry intended to divorce his wife circulated from time to time in the years before 1520, but no serious historian has treated them as more than diplomatic gossip that probably arose from comments made in moments of passing anger or disappointment at the failure of a pregnancy or the death of a baby. However, a number of writers have chosen to speculate that the firm intention to divorce was formed in 1524 or 1525, once Henry's medical advisers had informed him that the queen was unlikely to conceive again. This is not a totally implausible theory – certainly there is evidence that Henry was contemplating the possibility of divorce and remarriage as one of the options open to him in his quest for a male heir – but it is not the most likely scenario. The circumstantial evidence that weakens it most is that during this period Henry was seemingly grooming his illegitimate son, (born in 1519), whom he had created the Duke of Richmond and made the premier peer of the realm, to fill the role of heir-apparent. In these circumstances it is likely that the need to find a new wife would have been low on his list of priorities.

Most convincing – but by no means certain – is the suggestion that the king made up his mind at some time during 1527. It was then that it seems ('seems' because the evidence is by no means conclusive) he became besotted with Anne Boleyn, one of the young ladies at court and about 15 years his junior. Anne let him know that the attraction was mutual but that she would not become his sexual partner until she was also his wife. It took Henry some time to become convinced that this stance was more than courtly coyness and that the object of his desire intended to maintain her 'virtue' in the face of all the pressure that an English king could bring to bear on any female subject. It is probable that once the reality of the situation became clear to him and he also became aware that his infatuation was growing rather than diminishing, his mind turned increasingly to the doubts he had felt for some time about the validity of his marriage to Catherine.

These doubts revolved around a text from the Old Testament of the Bible (Leviticus chapter 20 verse 16) which read

> **If a man shall take his brother's wife, it is an impurity: he hath uncovered his brother's nakedness; they shall be childless.**

Henry was a quite accomplished amateur biblical scholar. This is apparent from the work he did on the book attacking the early teachings of Martin Luther which had been published in his name in 1521, and for which the Pope had awarded him the title of 'Defender of the Faith'. Therefore he would have been well able to recognise the force of the argument presented to him by one of his advisers (we do not know which or when, although Catherine was sure that it was Wolsey) that his lack of surviving legitimate male children was God's punishment for marrying in defiance of divine law. This was because Catherine had previously been married to Henry's elder brother Arthur, whose early death had made her a widow after five months of adolescent married life. It seems reasonable to surmise from what we know of Henry that his desire for Anne Boleyn led him speedily to convince himself that his marriage was against God's explicit commandment. Certainly, throughout his life he was regularly able to make himself genuinely believe that whatever he wanted to do was morally defensible. Thus the most plausible explanation of his decision to free himself of Catherine of Aragon, probably in 1527, appears to be lust justified by the moral certainty that he was currently living in sin and was therefore in danger of eternal damnation.

Although most people, at the time and subsequently, have found it difficult to take Henry's moral stance seriously, those with a deep understanding of the king's personality have generally concluded that his scruples were genuine. This view is substantiated by the lengths to which he went to convince others that he meant what he said and that he was not merely making a propaganda point. Edward Hall recorded that in November 1528 the king assembled at his palace of Bridewell [in London] his nobility, judges and counsellors, with various other persons, to whom he declared the great worthiness of his wife, both for her nobility and virtue and all princely qualities, to be such that if he were to marry again he would marry her of all women, if the marriage were found to be good and lawful. But, despite her worthiness and the fact that he had a fair daughter by her, he said that he was wonderfully tormented in his conscience, for he understood from many great clerks whom he had consulted, that he had lived all this time in detestable and abominable adultery. Therefore to settle his conscience, and the sure and firm succession of the realm ... he said that if by the law of God she should be judged to be his lawful wife, nothing would be more pleasant and acceptable to him in his whole life.

Once the decision had been made to seek a divorce, Henry must have thought that the action to be taken was straightforward and that success was guaranteed. It is probable that he shared his determination to separate himself from his queen in conversation with Wolsey at an early stage, and that his leading minister assured him that there would be no difficulty in meeting his requirements. What was needed was for the Pope to declare that the original papal dispensation allowing the marriage to take place was invalid, thus ruling that Henry and Catherine had never legally been man and wife and that the supposed marriage was annulled. Wolsey was confident that such an outcome would be speedily achieved. After all, such annulments were relatively commonplace (the Duke of Suffolk had required one to legalise his marriage to Henry's sister, Mary), and the Pope had every reason to please the ruler of a country whose support he often sought in his diplomatic manoeuvrings. In addition, Wolsey was one of the most influential men in the Church and was owed favours by many of those who advised the Pope on matters of policy.

2 The Initial Campaign

> **KEY ISSUES** What were the three approaches used by Cardinal Wolsey in his attempt to obtain a divorce for Henry? Why did each approach fail?

However, things did not go at all as planned. The attempt to persuade Rome to grant the annulment 'on the nod' was met by obvious stalling tactics, particularly the reference of key issues to groups of advisers who were clearly expected to take their time in formulating any recommendations. As the months passed by and nothing seemed to be happening, Henry's frustration, fanned by Anne Boleyn and her political allies, showed itself in heated outbursts to Wolsey and in demands for more forceful action to be taken. And so, what had been expected to be a matter of a little behind-the-scenes 'fixing', was turned into a very public confrontation between Henry and the Papacy.

In these circumstances Wolsey attempted to work on three fronts at once, expecting that one of them at least would be successful. He could hardly have done more. Two of the approaches required Rome to make the decision Henry wanted. The first involved persuading the Pope, both by reason and by exerting diplomatic pressure, that the original dispensation carried no force because popes had no right to set aside divine law, as the prohibition contained in Leviticus was claimed to be. Logical as this strategy might have seemed, it was politically very inept. No pope was ever likely to admit publicly that one of his recent predecessors had exceeded his powers. To make matters worse, theologians were very divided over many of the issues raised by the case. Not only were there divisions of opinion over whether the law laid down in Leviticus was open to papal dispensation, but there was even widespread disagreement over what the biblical instruction actually meant. There were many who argued that the intention was that a man should not marry his brother's wife while his brother was still living, but that once he was dead the prohibition lapsed. This line of argument appeared to be supported by an Old Testament text from the book of Deuteronomy which instructed that a man should marry his brother's widow if she was childless and should have children by her on his brother's behalf. The sensible approach might have been to abandon this line of attack once it had ceased to be clearcut. But Henry dug in his heels. He was certain that his theological interpretation was correct and he was determined that the world should see that it was so. In order to achieve this, numbers of leading theologians were paid large sums of money to write treatises supporting the 'English' view. But this did not suffice. An equally powerful sequence of books supporting the opposite point of view soon appeared. And it is generally judged that those who opposed Henry's interpretation – including Bishop Fisher of Rochester who made himself Catherine's leading defender and who published seven books arguing his case – came off best in the dispute. This first approach, supported by a number of fairly clumsy diplomatic initiatives, yielded at best inconclusive results. What was worse, it ensured that the case gained such a high international profile that it became almost impossible for the Papacy to give way without a huge loss of face.

The second approach initially appeared more promising because it involved no challenge to the powers of the Papacy. It was to object to the dispensation on technical grounds, by arguing that it was invalid – and that thus the marriage also was – because it was incorrectly worded. This line of argument seemed more likely to find favour in the Curia (the Papacy's administrative centre) because its acceptance would involve no more than an admission that a clerical error had been made. But Catherine of Aragon, who had been aware from the beginning what was happening, had no intention of allowing her marriage to be annulled if she could possibly help it. Her supporters and agents were soon busily at work and were fortunate enough to locate a slightly differently worded version of the dispensation among the royal papers in Spain. What is more, this newly discovered version sat-isfied the criteria which the copy held in England was argued not to. Much delay, and further frustration, was caused by Charles V (in his capacity as ruler of the Spanish kingdoms) refusing to allow the Spanish version to leave the country. Consequently, the second approach gradually lost its momentum.

Wolsey's third strategy was to attempt to persuade the Pope to allow the case to be decided in England. His real hope was that the decision would be delegated to the Pope's representative on the spot – Wolsey himself. It was thought that the Pope might favour such a solution as it would remove from him any personal involvement in the decision reached. On several occasions, when letters were received by Wolsey from his agents in Rome announcing that papers delegating authority in the way requested had been issued, it appeared that suc-cess was to come via this route. But each time euphoria was to be fol-lowed by disappointment as it was discovered on the papers' arrival that they were intentionally deficient in some respect. The normal problem was that the Pope was to retain a reserve power to accept or reject the judgement reached in England as he thought fit. As far as both Wolsey and Henry were concerned, such an arrangement was worse than useless in that it seemed to be no more than yet another stalling device.

However, a breakthrough seemed to have been achieved in 1528 when the Pope at last appeared to agree to a final decision being made in England. The compromise that the English were required to accept was that the judgement would be reached jointly by two papal legates – Cardinal Campeggio as well as Cardinal Wolsey. This arrangement seemed to threaten no danger to the English cause, as Wolsey had worked with Campeggio before (when negotiating the Treaty of London in 1518) and was confident that he would be able to 'manage' this partner whom the Pope was sending from Rome to join him. In addition, Campeggio was already in Henry's pay (as the absentee Bishop of Salisbury) to look after English interests in the Curia. The Pope's offer was therefore speedily accepted, and Henry's spirits rose at the prospect of the imminent resolution of his problem. Unfortunately for Wolsey's peace of mind, the king's frustration and impatience increased just as rapidly when it became clear that Campeggio did not share the English monarch's sense of urgency. It is true that he was in poor health and that the journey he had been instructed to undertake was therefore most unwelcome, but even in these circumstances his progress northwards was (literally) painfully slow. Frequent breaks were taken for recuperation, and, as these were reported in detail to Henry by his agents, each one worsened the king's temper considerably. And not surprisingly, given Henry's per-sonality, Wolsey was blamed for every new delay. Matters did not improve once Campeggio finally reached London in December 1528. The speedy decision that had been hoped for was not forthcoming as he insisted that everything be done 'according to the book'. Nothing that Wolsey could do was able to hurry the process as Campeggio proved impervious to all the pressures that normally ensured that Wolsey got his way. There was no threat and no offer that could influence the Roman cardinal for he was tired of life and had no aspirations for the future. His only motivation seemed to be to carry out the Pope's wishes and the fact that he was paid to work in England's interests appeared to be of no significance. Both Henry and Wolsey soon realised that they had been duped by what was probably yet another delaying tactic, and their suspicions were finally confirmed when work on the case was suspended in July 1529 without a decision being made. Campeggio was insisting that all activity cease for the long summer period during which the courts in Rome were in recess. All concerned realised then that Campeggio would never be prepared to commit himself to a verdict one way or the other. And so it proved. Before the hearing in England could be reconvened in the autumn, the Pope had decided that the case must, after all, be heard in Rome.

This decision was essentially the final nail in Wolsey's political coffin. For more than two years he had been promising a rapid and successful conclusion to the king's 'great matter'. Now it was clear that all his words had been worthless and a very angry Henry was at last prepared to believe the arguments that Anne Boleyn and her faction had been advancing for many months – that the king's chief minister was as responsible for the lack of action as were the men in Rome. It was ironic that Wolsey's arrest and fall from power in October 1529 took place when it did, because at that time he would have been jointly presiding over the continuation of the hearing of the king's case if the Pope had not called the proceedings to a halt.

3 Wolsey's Failure

> **KEY ISSUE** How far was Wolsey responsible for Henry's failure between 1527 and 1529 to have his marriage annulled?

The lack of conclusive evidence has resulted in historians disagreeing about the part Wolsey played in the failure to secure the king the divorce he so desperately desired. However, the balance of probability now seems to be fairly firmly established. Those who have seen Wolsey as the secret saboteur of the king's plans are probably correct in their assessment of the Cardinal's personal feelings about the divorce and the outcome he hoped to see. Their claim is that Anne Boleyn was essentially accurate in her judgement that Wolsey was hostile to her and her cause. There is certainly impressive evidence that there was no love lost between these two very forceful personalities, and that the minister resented the influence the king's second-wife-in-waiting exercised in the political arena. It is almost self-evident that Wolsey had nothing to gain and much to lose from the replacement of Catherine of Aragon (who played little part in day-to-day politics) by Anne Boleyn (who made no secret of the fact that she expected to be the king's *confidante* in all matters of importance). It was not that he feared a change of policy: rather that he correctly foresaw a significant diminution in his own power and influence if the divorce and remarriage were to go ahead. Thus, it was naturally his hope that the problem would just go away – presumably by Henry tiring of Anne Boleyn and deciding that he would rather leave things as they were. And there was every reason to believe that this would be the most likely outcome. Wolsey had plenty of experience of the king's enthusiasms, which tended to be all-consuming but short-lived, and he knew that the best way of dealing with them was to appear to go along with them until they ran out of steam in the normal course of events.

However, those who have gone on from this to argue that Wolsey acted for most of the time between 1527 and 1529 in line with his personal preferences have been less persuasive. They have managed to show that occasionally the Cardinal was less energetic than he would have been had his heart been fully in the divorce project, but they have been unable to establish that he was consistently so. In addition, they have found only one example of him taking action that could be interpreted as being designed to make the divorce less likely to happen. This was when he changed his initial view that the matter could be dealt with by the Church hierarchy in England to a strongly stated opinion that only the Pope could give the necessary rulings. It is reasonable to suggest that Wolsey, who was not slow to exceed his powers in other matters, would only have done this had his intention been to bog down the matter in the bureaucratic quagmire of Rome. But the case is by no means proven because, on the other hand, it is equally convincing to argue that, in doing this Wolsey was merely protecting himself against difficulties that might have arisen in the future had opponents challenged the validity of a verdict reached in England and thus thrown the legitimacy of any children born to Henry and Anne into doubt.

But the most compelling reason for not accepting the interpretation that Wolsey consistently worked against the divorce, (in addition to opposing it privately), is the clear evidence that he soon came to realise that his political future depended on the king's marriage to Catherine of Aragon being dissolved. Some of his letters to Rome reveal a man who was desperately fighting for his survival and who was even prepared to plead for action in order to save his skin. The air of desperation that surrounded so much of his diplomatic activity in 1528 and 1529, when he was attempting to exert pressure on the Pope to reach an early and favourable decision, does not smack of a man who was merely going through the motions until a change of heart on the part of his monarch freed him from his torment. Thus it seems probable that Wolsey failed to achieve his objective (with which he admittedly had no personal sympathy) despite the fact that he tried hard to be successful and not because he was secretly undermining his public endeavours.

4 The Years of Drift

> **KEY ISSUE** Were the years 1530 and 1531 'years of drift' as far as ending Henry's marriage with Catherine of Aragon was concerned?

1530 and 1531 have normally been described as years during which the campaign to obtain the divorce was conducted in an aimless fashion, with no clear strategy being apparent. It has been likened to a rudderless ship at sea in a storm. In this highly critical portrayal the failure has been seen as being both Henry's and that of his three leading ministers – the Dukes of Norfolk and Suffolk and the Earl of Wiltshire (Anne Boleyn's recently enobled father). These years have frequently been taken as proving that, whatever other qualities and strengths he might have possessed, the king was no strategist and no 'man of business'. In particular, those who have wanted to show that Henry was as dependent on able ministers as they were on him have made much of the sterility of the period between the fall of Wolsey and the rise of Cromwell. Certainly, there has been no difficulty in establishing that Norfolk, Suffolk and Wiltshire probably had less political acumen between them than even any one of Wolsey's team of 'lieutenants' (which, of course, included Thomas Cromwell) had on his own.

However, this picture is possibly a little harsh on Henry. At least one major initiative was taken in an attempt to win a victory in the debates on the meaning of the Leviticus text and on the Pope's power to issue a dispensation for a man to marry his brother's widow. Henry had already procured an amount of learned support for his case, but now a concerted effort was made to secure formal 'judgements' on the issue from the most prestigious universities of Europe. Large sums of money were spent bribing theologians to vote in Henry's favour and ten verdicts were obtained. But the overall impact of the campaign was minimal, especially as it was widely known that gold rather than conscience had decided many of the outcomes. Some of the participants were even prepared to be bribed by Catherine of Aragon's party (two payments rather than one) to declare publicly that they really believed the dispensation to be valid and that they had only said otherwise because they had been paid to do so. In such ways the credibility of the exercise – which had never been high – was almost totally destroyed.

Yet, unsuccessful as the venture was, it does not seem to indicate a policy without a sense of direction. But it does suggest that the approach being adopted was a mere elaboration of the failed strategy that Wolsey had attempted to implement. The aim was still to persuade the Pope to declare in Henry's favour by convincing him of the rightness of the king's case, despite the clear-cut evidence that the Curia was likely neither to be swayed by public opinion, however eminent were its spokesmen, nor unduly influenced by the facts of the case, one way or the other. Henry's agenda and Rome's agenda were poles apart.

But at least these years witnessed one success of sorts. The great fear in London, after the case had been revoked to Rome in the summer of 1529, had been that a verdict in favour of Catherine would be issued. So the English agents in Italy were instructed to reverse the direction of their efforts, and instead of trying to speed up the process they were told to slow it down as much as possible. They undoubtedly managed to initiate some additional delays in what was already a very slow and complicated process, but it is unlikely that, even without their work, any final decision would have been forthcoming for a very long time. Thus there is little credit to be claimed for achieving the 'success', even though the worst outcome had not come about.

So it seems that the 'flavour' of the writers who have judged the time after Wolsey's fall to be the wasted years is correct, even if their case has sometimes been overstated in an attempt to show that a Henry poorly advised was a king who was all at sea. Certainly it would be fair to describe 1530 and 1531, as far as the divorce was concerned, as a period when no strategy that could reasonably have been expected to lead to a successful conclusion to the affair was being pursued. Nobody seemed able to identify the way forward.

5 The Breakthrough

KEY ISSUES What idea provided the breakthrough? What was done to implement the idea?

Rarely is it possible in history to credit anybody with a completely new idea. The greatness of the men and women who have made important discoveries, pioneered new approaches, or carried through significant changes has normally been based on the ability to draw together a number of existing ideas and to refashion them into a way of looking at things that had not been apparent before. The process is so simple that most 'new' good ideas seem so obvious once someone else has thought of them. Probably at some time in 1531, Thomas

Cromwell hit upon such a new good idea about the divorce. It was that the Pope would never be prevailed upon to rule in Henry's favour and that the only way forward was to remove the power in such matters from the Pope's hands and to give it to someone or some group willing to be persuaded by the king.

Cromwell's strength was that besides being able to describe clearly *what* needed to be done he was also able both to indicate *how* it could be done and to guarantee to do it himself. It seems that, although Henry was quick to recognise the talent of this relatively low-born former lieutenant of his fallen minister and to see that he was a man whose services should be used, he was unwilling to accept the total package that was on offer. It was necessary to persuade him of its good sense and practicality little by little. Therefore there was no sudden change of direction leading to speedy success: rather there was an edging towards a new way forward. This was done with much wavering and hesitation, until events almost took on a momentum of their own and the breakthrough was achieved.

The key decision was to use parliament to pass laws restricting papal powers by recognising that these powers in fact resided in the Crown of England, and stipulating the punishments that would be meted out to those who opposed or acted contrary to the new arrangements. It is difficult for us, who have grown up in a democracy where parliament has been supreme for centuries, to appreciate the brilliance of the approach suggested by Cromwell and accepted by Henry. At the time it was generally accepted that parliament was a rarely and briefly used component of political life (it had played no significant part in the first 20 years of Henry's reign) whose main functions were to grant extraordinary taxes to the king in times of great national need and to pass new laws covering mainly minor local issues. The idea of using it to bring about a revolution in the relationship between Church and State was highly innovative. It was also very shrewd. It ensured that the representatives of the landed and merchant classes, upon whom the king depended to exercise his authority throughout the country, would be fully implicated in whatever was done.

The crucial action was the passage of the Act in Restraint of Appeals in March 1533. This legislation declared that final authority in all legal matters, lay and clerical, resided in the monarch and that it was therefore illegal to appeal to any authority outside the kingdom on any such matters (for a fuller treatment of this and associated acts see pages 43–4). The way was now clear for the validity of Henry and Catherine's marriage to be decided finally without the involvement of the Pope or his bureaucracy. And the people were in place who could be relied on to carry out the work speedily and with the desired outcome. In particular, there was a new Archbishop of Canterbury, the head of the Church hierarchy in England and Wales. The old archbishop, William Warham, who had taken great pleasure in outliving

Cardinal Wolsey so that he could prevent the man he so greatly detested adding Canterbury to his many other clerical positions, had finally died in 1532. While he had lived there had always been the possibility that he would summon up enough courage to refuse to do as he was directed by Henry. Certainly, he was not in favour of the divorce and he had proved himself willing to be obstructive to the king, even if his resolve had normally crumbled once pressure had been applied. But with the old man dead, the way was clear for Henry to choose a totally pliable replacement (as long as the Pope could be prevailed upon to endorse the man chosen).

The choice fell on Thomas Cranmer who appeared to have all the right attributes. He had shown a marked lack of personal ambition during the 43 or so years of his life so far, much of which had been spent at Cambridge quietly studying and teaching. But he was intellectually very able and had shown himself to be strongly in favour of the divorce. He had already been useful to the king, carrying out his instructions to the letter, whether it was in writing a book supporting Henry's case (in 1529), acting as an agent buying support in European universities (in 1530), or (as now) serving as England's ambassador at the court of Charles V. In addition, he was a very junior member of the Boleyn faction and was thus totally acceptable to Queen Anne-to-be. The only slight problem was that he held no position within the clerical hierarchy, although he was an ordained priest, and it might have proved difficult to justify the meteoric rise of such an outsider when no non-bishop had been elevated to Canterbury for well over a century. But Henry took the plunge and much to his relief the Pope, anxious to prove that he could please in some things, confirmed the appointment in record time.

Once the Act in Restraint of Appeals had become law there was a need for rapid action. Anne Boleyn, convinced that the divorce would soon be achieved, had finally consented to share her monarch's bed at some time in 1532. By January 1533 she knew that she was pregnant, and Cranmer was instructed to perform a secret marriage ceremony. It was now important that the divorce be finalised and the new marriage declared legal before the baby (hopefully a boy) was born in the early autumn. Cranmer acted with speed, tact and efficiency. A hearing of the case was arranged for late May and when Catherine refused to attend a judgement was delivered after less than three days of deliberation. It was announced that the papal dispensation had been invalid, that Henry and Catherine had therefore never been legally married, and that the secret marriage of Henry and Anne was in order because Henry had been a bachelor at the time. The king was well satisfied and was not in the least displeased that six years of endeavour on his 'great matter' had ended in such a tame and low-key victory. The anti-climax was to come when the baby turned out to be a girl!

6 Actions and Motives

Although there has been some dispute between historians over matters of detail, there is now general agreement about what happened between 1527 and 1533 in the efforts to secure the divorce and in its final achievement. What has intrigued (and divided) historians much more is the attempt to provide explanations about why events turned out as they did. In particular, the roles and motives of the main participants have been much discussed.

a) Charles V

KEY ISSUES What have Charles V's motives traditionally been interpreted as being in the action he took over Henry VIII's attempts to end his marriage to Catherine of Aragon? In what way does this interpretation need to be amended?

The vast majority of writers have judged that the most important person in influencing the outcome of Henry's 'great matter', in the years during which the King of England accepted that the decision on his marital fate lay with the Pope in Rome, was a person not mentioned in this chapter so far – the Emperor Charles V. The orthodox view has long been that Charles stopped the Pope from reaching a conclusion that was against the interests of Catherine of Aragon – mainly by making him fear what would happen to him if he did. It has been said that Charles V did this because Catherine was his aunt (his mother's sister) and that his strong sense of family pride drove him to do all he could to protect the honour of such a close relative. In addition, it has often been claimed that Catherine was one of his special favourites and that affection increased his already strong resolve.

With a motive so clearly established, there has been no difficulty in explaining how Charles was able to put his intention into effect. This was possible because, throughout the period 1527 to 1532, the Papacy was diplomatically and militarily at his mercy. The most striking example of this control took place in 1527 when Rome was overrun by his troops and was looted and pillaged for a fortnight with great ferocity. As a result of this unintended action by the Emperor's unpaid and mutinous German soldiers, the Pope, in effect, became for several months Charles's prisoner. Even when papal freedom was restored, the clear message remained that any hostile action would almost certainly be followed by unpleasant repercussions. In similar circumstances, which had occurred several times before during the 30 years of struggle between France and Spain for the control of Italy, papal policy had been predictable. An alliance had been formed with the temporary underdog (France or Spain) and as many other states as could be persuaded to fight to re-establish a balance of power in which they, and the Papacy, could once again exercise some independent influence. But on this occasion the strategy rapidly backfired. A hastily gathered consortium of states, including England and reliant on the military might of France, was discomfited in 1529 when the Emperor's armies were overwhelmingly victorious in battle and Charles was left the undisputed master of Italy. The Pope could now do little but squirm. And, although he could not be forced to take action against his will, he could be prevented from doing anything of which the Emperor did not approve. This, it has traditionally been argued, included granting Henry his divorce.

It is somewhat surprising that nearly all English-speaking writers about the divorce have accepted this account seemingly uncritically. For, although it rings true in general terms, it appears to be a very simplistic, and therefore partial, explanation of Charles's motives and role. Certainly, his motives are unlikely to have been as straightforward as they are normally portrayed as having been. It is true that he was a committed dynast who was determined to hand on in their entirety the lands and powers he had inherited if he possibly could, and that he made constant use of his relations to help him control his huge and scattered personal empire. But how well he protected (and by implication wished to) their individual interests is more open to question. There are clear cases where he did not, especially where it suited him politically not to. The most obvious example is of his mother (Catherine of Aragon's sister) through whom he had inherited the Spanish kingdoms and their empires. Her claims to rule were passed over in Charles's favour and for most of his life she 'existed' in splendid captivity – and all because of her supposed madness brought on by the sudden death of her husband. It is uncontestable that 'madder' male monarchs had often been allowed to rule and that her son showed scant concern for her welfare. Equally, there is little evidence that he cared for Catherine of Aragon in personal terms. Not only did he hardly know her, but he seemingly made no attempt to better the acquaintance during his visits to England. Thus any claim that she was a special favourite of his seems to have very little justification.

Nor was Charles particularly sensitive to slurs that were cast on his family name, unless it suited him to appear so. He kept his ears firmly closed to the appeals of another aunt when she was 'thrown over' by her royal husband – the King of Denmark – in circumstances that were not totally dissimilar to those affecting Catherine of Aragon. And he did nothing to right the wrongs done to his supposed 'favourite aunt' in the three years between her divorce and her death. In fact, he was very quick to forgive, forget and make up with Henry VIII when it suited him to do so.

Thus it appears that further work needs to be done to disentangle Charles V's reasons for opposing the divorce as strenuously as he undoubtedly did. The answer is likely to lie in a mixture of political self-interest and personal pride. For example, once he had declared himself opposed to the divorce, and once the issue had became a matter of widespread international debate, it is possible that his determination not to be worsted by his highly competitive and often patronising uncle-in-law became the key issue for him. However, many readers will be able to construct hypotheses that are just as plausible as this – and they will be safe to do so in the knowledge that the 'experts' have yet to establish a convincing explanation.

Equally, the orthodox view that 'Charles V opposed the divorce and that therefore the Pope could not grant it' seems open to challenge. At least it appears valid to contend that the Pope could have acted had he wanted to (at a price), just as he did in 1528 when he allied with Henry VIII and others in a foolhardy attempt to loosen the emperor's grip on Italy. Certainly, the Pope was much more than a pawn in the game.

b) The Pope

> **KEY ISSUES** What have the Pope's motives traditionally been interpreted as being in the action he took over Henry VIII's attempts to end his marriage to Catherine of Aragon? In what way does this interpretation need to be amended?

During the whole of the struggle over the divorce the Pope was the same person – Clement VII (1523–34). He was in many ways a pathetic figure. The abiding image of him when dealing with the divorce is the description given by one English envoy of a dithering and distressed old man, wringing his hands in anguish and asking plaintively 'What shall I do?'. But his question was not really a request for guidance. He had plenty of that and he did not relish the implications of any of it. Everything that was suggested to him seemed guaranteed to make the situation worse. Whenever he was prevailed upon to do anything affecting the case he was immediately assailed by doubts about the decision he had just made. His normal response was to back-track, at least in part, as quickly as he could. Intense frustration was therefore the lot of those who had to deal with him on the matter.

However, Clement was not consistently indecisive. There were times when he displayed an amazing amount of inner strength and outward certainty. After the Sack of Rome in 1527, and again a year later, he was persistent in his determination not to act as a tool of the emperor. He was equally determined not to be bullied by the King of England. These underlying resolves seem never to have deserted him and to have been present even during the periods of weakness when he appeared to be too frightened of everyone and everything to make any decisions at all. Thus, the man who looked as if he ought to be easily manipulated turned out to be unmanageable.

From what he said and did it appears that Clement resented the divorce issue greatly. He looked upon it as a most unwelcome and insoluble problem, and one that had been thrust on him through no fault of his own. His fervent wish was that it would go away without him having to do anything, although he was hopeful that Catherine would be treated fairly. This could happen by one of the parties dying (not an unreasonable option in an age when life was often short), by Henry tiring of Anne Boleyn and deciding to drop the issue (a distinct possibility given the temporary nature of most infatuations), or by the English taking the law into their own hands. Clement is reported on several occasions as wishing that this would happen. Certainly, it had been done many times before as a face-saving exercise. In Henry's case it would have meant him marrying Anne Boleyn without having secured an annulment of his existing marriage, and then at some appropriate time in the future (probably after Catherine's death) applying to the Pope for his situation to be regularised and for his children by his second wife to be declared legitimate. It would probably have been possible to do this without difficulty. One other frequently used solution to such problems was suggested as events unfolded. This was to persuade Catherine to enter a nunnery, thus freeing her husband to marry again if he wished. Campeggio arrived in England in 1528 with the instruction to inform Catherine that the Pope advised this. Catherine's response was typically spirited. She thought it was an excellent suggestion which she would be pleased to accept once Henry agreed to enter a monastery!

Much as Clement was vacillating and despondent, hoping to avoid all responsibility over the affair, he was consistent in his determination that no verdict should be forthcoming from Rome while there was still a possibility that the dispute would be settled by other means. Thus, for him, the strategy to be pursued was clear-cut. Delay must be the order of the day, with minimal (and, if possible, illusory) concessions being made only when the pressure on him became intense. So, although he eventually agreed to the case being decided in England, he ensured that Campeggio was in no doubt that under no circumstances must a conclusion be reached. His final ruling, made in Catherine's favour just before he died in 1534, was only issued because Henry had very much taken the law into his own hands by then.

c) Henry VIII

KEY ISSUES What have Henry VIII's motives traditionally been interpreted as being in the action he took in the attempt to end his marriage to Catherine of Aragon? In what way does this interpretation need to be amended?

Henry's motives over his 'great matter' are normally presented as a mixture of lust for Anne Boleyn and concern to provide himself with an acceptable male heir. But, important as these factors were, it would clearly be unrealistic to expect such simple statements fully to reflect the intentions of such a complex and changeable king over a six–year period.

Contemporaries were amazed that his passion for Anne could remain at such a pitch for so long. The most popular explanation for this untypical constancy was that she had used black magic to bewitch him. This was not as ridiculous a suggestion as it may now seem, because in sixteenth-century England many of the unusual happenings in life were habitually put down to the effects of witchcraft. In reality, Anne did manage her relationship with Henry very skilfully indeed. She made mistakes – especially, on occasions, continuing to press a point beyond the time when the king wished to hear about it – but generally her touch was sure. She worked hard to be good company for him whatever his mood, and she inflamed his passions from time to time by those displays of courtly eroticism which were an accepted part of early modern life in the highest Western European societies. She was careful to make certain that he did not forget what would be his once he was able to offer his hand in marriage! However, it would be inaccurate to think that Henry was consumed by lust throughout the struggle with Rome. His sex drive was insufficiently strong for this to be so, and his affection for Anne had very clear limits. He undoubtedly held concern over his own health as a higher priority than being with the one he loved. He was quick to send her away from court when there was a suspicion that she might be affected by the sweating sickness, a disease that he feared more than anything else. Equally, his departure from London, leaving Anne behind, was very speedy whenever an outbreak of the disease occurred there. Observers at the time were correct in assessing that Anne was of lasting importance in their king's life, but some historians have perhaps been lured by them into exaggerating her role as a driving force behind Henry's actions throughout the struggle for the divorce. The king's love for her was deep and enduring but it only intermittently provided the major motivation for his actions.

The same could be argued even more strongly over Henry's desire to procure a legitimate male heir. There is no doubt that this was an issue which concerned him, but there is little evidence that it was at the forefront of his mind except in the months after January 1533 when Anne had told him she was pregnant. Then it was definitely the most important single factor in driving him towards a speedy resolution of the matter whatever the cost. At other times it was probably no more than a background contributory factor which helped to strengthen his resolve. But it would be very difficult to construct a defensible argument in support of a contention that it was an issue of vital importance.

If the most frequently offered explanations of Henry's motivation are important but overall not the *most* important, what then spurred him on over such a long time when he was beset with so many difficulties in continuing with the campaign to have his marriage annulled? In small part, the answer is that often the effort was maintained in response to a combination of motivating forces, including the two already discussed, rather than based on a single all-important factor, and that these combinations varied from day to day and even from hour to hour, depending on what was said to the king and on how he was feeling. Too little has often been made of this variety of factors. It has been common to ignore Henry's sense of guilt over the sinfulness of his marriage which, although self-inspired, was none-the-less ever present and ready to be activated by those who wished to bolster his determination. Equally overlooked has been his ever-deepening and irrational hatred of Catherine as the cause of all his problems, which led him to wish to exact revenge on her as fully as possible. In addition, there was the genuine interest created by the campaign to establish control over the Church within England and Wales which probably began in 1531 (see page 34) and which kept him fully committed to the campaign.

However, there was a single factor that seems to have dominated Henry's motivation for a significant part of the time, at least after the early stages of the enterprise. This was the determination to be seen to be right in the stand he had taken over the status of his marriage. The other side of this coin was that he would do everything possible to prevent it looking as if he had come off second best in a struggle with Charles V. This became an enormous point of honour with him – all the more so as he was used to being told by others that he was right and to getting his own way in almost every matter. And the longer the dispute continued and the more public it became, the less acceptable would have been his loss of face had he been seen to give way. It is not possible to identify for certain a date by which Henry was irrevocably committed to obtaining a successful outcome to the venture, but he had definitely placed himself in a position from which there was no going back by the time Cardinal Campeggio had left the country after the abortive legatine court in 1529. Only for such a reason would this pleasure-loving king have allowed a single 'political' issue to have engrossed almost all his attention for months at a time.

This motivation also offers a credible explanation for his maintaining a frontal attack on Clement VII for five unbroken years – long after any uncommitted observer would have judged there to be any realistic chance of success – instead of accepting the 'back door' solution of a clandestine marriage to Anne, as it had been broadly hinted to him that the Pope thought he should. It might also be one of the reasons why he was never prepared to contemplate the other easy way out – the murder of Catherine of Aragon. Such solutions were by no means rare in the early sixteenth century, when the poisoner's art was well developed. Certainly, Catherine's closest friends feared that such would be her fate, and when she eventually died in 1536 there were many who believed, quite mistakenly it seems, that her death was not by natural causes. In addition, Henry is known on occasions to have commissioned assassins to rid him of opponents whom he could not deal with openly, so he clearly did not object to such methods on principle. There is definitely good reason to believe that for Henry the means by which he was seen to achieve his success was apparently as important as the fact that he obtained his divorce. At least this was so until Anne's pregnancy dictated that a speedy solution must take precedence over one which was resplendent in public celebration of his rightful victory. Perhaps this is part of the reason why he made Anne's coronation a 'no expenses spared' affair only a week or so later.

d) Catherine of Aragon

> **KEY ISSUES** What judgement has traditionally been made of the way Catherine of Aragon acted over Henry VIII's attempts to have their marriage annulled? To what extent does this judgement need to be modified?

Had the queen been prepared to 'go quietly', the divorce would not have been the long-running international scandal that it became. However, Catherine was anything but an Anne of Cleves (four wives later), who was almost pleased to have her marriage annulled in return for a comfortable and trouble-free existence. The first queen was made of much sterner stuff. Henry was surprised as well as infuriated by the unmoveable stand that she took, for Catherine had always previously acted as the ideal, (from Henry's point of view), submissive wife, accepting her husband's periodic infidelities and more frequent inattentiveness with a good grace and without altering her bearing towards him. But she drew a very definite line when the legality of her long years of marriage (since 1509) and the legitimacy of her only surviving child (Mary) were challenged.

Catherine's position began and remained very clear-cut. As far as she was concerned, there could be no doubts about the validity of her marriage to Henry. She knew that she had been a virgin at the time of her second marriage (although others disputed the fact), she was certain that the Pope's dispensation had removed any impediment that her unconsumated marriage to Arthur might have placed in the way of her legally becoming Henry's wife, and she could see no reason why a marriage that had remained unquestioned for 19 years should now be disputed. In addition and in all modesty, she believed that she had been a very good wife and consort to her royal husband and she felt strongly that natural justice demanded she be allowed to continue

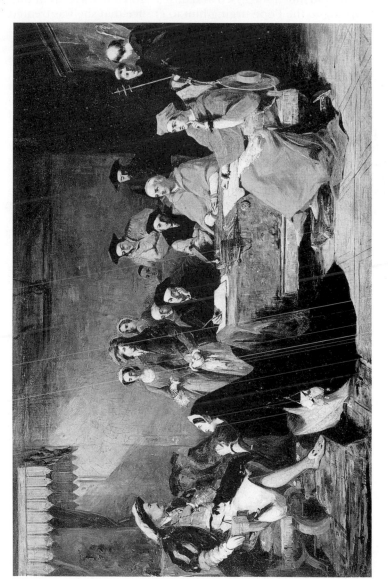

'The Trial of Catherine of Aragon', painted by Henry Nelson O'Neil in the nineteenth century.

in this role. This feeling was so strong that she considered herself justified in opposing her husband over the question of the annulment. It was this *active* opposition (rather than the passive resistance he had expected) that so much surprised and infuriated Henry. He knew that she was writing to the Pope urging him to ensure that she was treated justly in the matter, and that she was in frequent correspondence with Charles V pleading with him to put pressure on the Pope in her interest. But, try as he would, he was unable to block all her channels of communication. Nor was he able to prevent her from winning public relations victories in the contest. The greatest of these was during her appearance before Campeggio and Wolsey's legatine court in June 1529 (she won additional respect by refusing to attend or to be represented at any of the other legal proceedings that Henry initiated in England). Breaking all the rules of procedure, she approached Henry and, on bended knee, pleaded with him to treat her justly and to abandon his attempts to secure an annulment. She then swept from the court, with the judges' demands that she remain ringing in her ears. The king was reportedly nonplussed, while most of the others present were highly impressed. Perhaps Catherine even surprised herself by the boldness of her actions. Edward Hall reported that:

1   the queen would remain no longer to hear what they [the legates] would further decide even though the king also asked and commanded her to stay, about which she seemed afterwards to suffer some remorse, as for some disobedience towards her husband. And she
5   reported afterwards to some who were then her counsellors (from whom I heard of it) that she had never before in her life in anything in the world disobeyed the king, her husband, and she would not have done so now, but the necessary defence of her cause forced her to.

William Shakespeare, who knew how to make the most of any dramatic situation, ensured that the incident became a firm part of the English literary tradition. In his last play, *Henry VIII*, written over 80 years after the events he described, he had Catherine say:

1   Sir, I desire you do me right and justice
And to bestow your pity on me; for
I am a most poor woman, and a stranger,
Born out of your dominions; having here
5   No judge indifferent, nor no more assurance
Of equal friendship and proceeding. Alas, Sir,
In what have I offended you? What cause
Hath my behaviour given to your displeasure,
That thus you should proceed to put me off,
10 And take your good grace from me? Heaven witness,
I have been to you a true and humble wife,
At all times to your will conformable;
Ever in fear to kindle your dislike,

Yea, subject to your countenance, – glad or sorry,
15 As I saw it inclined. When was the hour
I ever contradicted your desire,
Or made it not mine too? ...

Sympathetic writers – and most historians have fallen into this category – have commented very favourably on the way in which Catherine conducted herself throughout the divorce campaign and afterwards. Not only did she maintain her dignity in all situations, including a successful resistance to her forced removal from one 'home' to another, but she also set herself strict limits to the nature of her opposition to her husband. She refused ever to say or to write anything that was a direct criticism of him and she declined to be associated with any plan that might result in violence. This was particularly important during the last three years of her life when Eustace Chapuys, Charles V's ambassador in England, was attempting to organise a rebellion on her behalf and to persuade his master to send troops to bolster the native insurgents. Catherine even wrote to her nephew asking him not to listen to such advice.

It is normally said that Catherine was the only person to emerge from the divorce campaign with an enhanced reputation. It is easy to understand why this is so. It is also claimed that her popularity within England was widespread and deep-felt. The spirit of this assessment is accurate, despite the fact that in all likelihood it has been exaggerated somewhat. The most readily available source of evidence about the state of public opinion after 1529 is the large collection of Eustace Chapuys' detailed reports to Charles V, which has long been used by English historians when researching the subject. But sufficient account has not always been taken of the fact that Chapuys was often at pains to stress Catherine's popularity in order to persuade the emperor that if he invaded England he would receive large-scale local support. Perhaps it would be healthier if his judgements had been assessed more critically than they often have been.

However, the fact remains – substantiated from many other sources – that Catherine was generally thought to have been ill-treated and that, once Wolsey was dead, Henry attracted much of the blame for this. But the significance of the Dowager Duchess of Wales, as Henry insisted Catherine be addressed after the annulment of her second marriage, was much greater than her role as the initial cause of the king's growing unpopularity. Unwittingly, she was a major cause of the Reformation in England, because, had her husband not been determined to sever his ties to her, it is very unlikely that the break with Rome would have occurred – at least during the reign of Henry VIII.

Summary Diagram
The Divorce

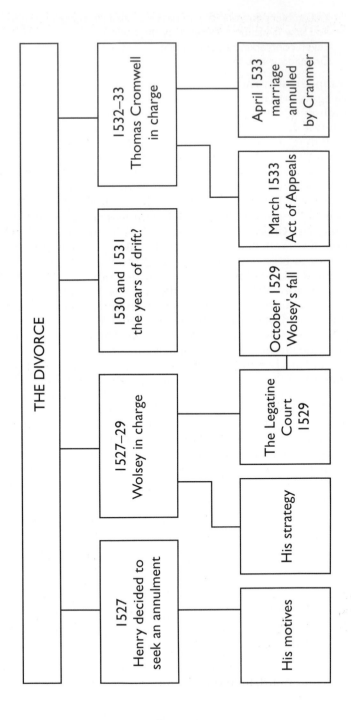

THE DIVORCE

1527
Henry decided to
seek an annulment

1527–29
Wolsey in charge

1530 and 1531
the years of drift?

1532–33
Thomas Cromwell
in charge

His motives

His strategy

The Legatine
Court
1529

October 1529
Wolsey's fall

March 1533
Act of Appeals

April 1533
marriage
annulled
by Cranmer

Working on Chapter 2

Two tasks are essential:

i) to construct a chronological outline of the main events between 1527 and 1533, and
ii) to reach conclusions about the motives of the main 'players' in the dispute (especially Henry VIII).

The first task can best be done by copying out the entries in the Key Dates list at the beginning of the chapter and, in each case, adding a sentence or two to explain why the event is considered to be significant.

When you are working on the second task it would be worthwhile concentrating on the way in which interpretations and judgements have changed and/or need to change. Then, in an examination answer, you will be able to show that you clearly understand the nature of historical uncertainty – that there are few 'right' answers to historical problems, and that what we have is interpretations that are more convincing or less convincing.

If you have already constructed a set of notes on Thomas Wolsey, it would be a good idea to add a section on 'The Divorce' to them.

Answering structured and essay questions on Chapter 2

Examine this two-part question:

a) Between 1527 and 1533 what action did Henry VIII take in an attempt to end his marriage to Catherine of Aragon?
b) Why was he unsuccessful in his attempts?

As always with structured questions, it is vital to identify what sort of written answer each part of the question requires of you. In this example one part is asking for a narrative of events and the other demands an explanation. Which part is which? When you give an explanation of the type required here you need to do two things. The obvious one is that you must describe a number of different causes. The less obvious one is that you must make a judgement about the relative importance of each cause. You need to have a pre-planned method of deciding relative importance. If you are not confident you have this, perhaps now is a good time to discuss the issue with your teacher and/or your fellow students. But before you do, read the rest of this section.

As you know, it is very rare for an essay question to be set on a topic as limited in scope as the divorce. Those that do appear tend to be straightforward, following the time-honoured principle that questions covering a very restricted and specified subject area are challenging enough already without the difficulty being compounded by the use of wording that requires a significant amount of 'unpacking'.

Typical examples of such questions are:

1. Why did Henry VIII find it so difficult to obtain a divorce from Catherine of Aragon? and
2. How far was Cardinal Wolsey responsible for Henry VIII's failure in his 'great matter' up to the end of 1529?

But beware! Some questions that seem to be about the divorce are really about much more and could only be answered satisfactorily by using ideas and information from both this and the next chapter. Identify which of the following examples fall into this category.

3. Discuss the view that 'the divorce was the occasion rather than the cause of the English Reformation'.
4. What were the consequences of the Pope's refusal to annul the marriage of Henry VIII and Catherine of Aragon?
5. Why did Henry VIII wish to terminate his marriage to Catherine of Aragon?

You will probably be well used to receiving the advice that the best way to begin planning an answer to a 'Why?' question, such as 1 and 5 above, is to draw up a number of 'because' statements, each of which can serve as a paragraph point. You may also have been told about the danger of producing an undifferentiated series of arguments, with the examiner being left wondering about the relative significance of the causes you describe. The obvious way to avoid this trap is to make sure that you rank the points you make in order of importance – probably beginning your essay with the most important and ending with the least significant.

Sometimes it is possible to rank causes according to quantity – the amount of money each cost for example – but this only happens infrequently. Certainly it would not work with questions 1 and 5 above. On most occasions, therefore, it is necessary to select a different criterion by which to order the causes. The most helpful technique is one which happens to allow the causes to be divided into two groups – the more important and the less important. This is done by asking the question, 'Would the event have happened if this had not been the case?' of each of the causes. If the answer is 'Yes', the cause is placed into the 'less important' category, but if the answer is 'No' the cause is a *sine qua non* (the Latin for 'without this it would not have happened') and is to be regarded as vital. There is frequently only one cause with a 'No' answer and, in such cases, that cause automatically becomes the main point of your essay. Very often it is sufficient to apply just this one criterion for ranking, with less important causes being presented in random order.

It would be a good idea to try out the *sine qua non* criterion on one or two questions. A workable essay plan would emerge if you apply the criterion to either question 1 or question 5.

Source-based questions on Chapter 2

1. The Bible and the Divorce

Carefully read the verse from Leviticus (page 11) and Hall's account of the meeting at the Bridewell in 1528 (page 11). Answer the following questions.

a) In what way was the verse from Leviticus open to different interpretations? How was this significant in Henry VIII's case? (*3 marks*)

b) What in the second extract could be used to suggest that the verse from Leviticus did not apply to Henry and Catherine's marriage? (*2 marks*)

c) Does the second extract provide indirect evidence that Catherine of Aragon was generally i) popular or ii) unpopular? Explain your answer. (*5 marks*)

d) What light does the second extract shed on i) Henry VIII's personality and character, and ii) his motives for seeking a divorce? (*5 marks*)

e) Using your own knowledge, explain why all those involved in deciding on the validity of Henry and Catherine's marriage paid so much attention to the exact wording of the Bible. (*15 marks*)

2. Catherine of Aragon and the Divorce

Carefully read the extracts from Edward Hall's *Chronicle*, given on page 28, and from William Shakespeare's *Henry VIII*, given on page 28 and study Henry Nelson O'Neil's nineteenth-century painting of 'The Trial of Catherine of Aragon' reproduced on page 27. Answer the following questions.

a) Why would Henry VIII have been surprised by the way in which Catherine acted, as described by Hall? (*4 marks*)

b) Did Hall give the impression that Catherine would have acted differently if she had been placed in the same position again? Explain your answer in detail. (*6 marks*)

c) What reaction is Shakespeare attempting to elicit from his audience? What techniques did he employ in doing this? (*5 marks*)

d) What reaction was O'Neil attempting to elicit from his audience? Illustrate your answer with descriptions of details from the painting. (*5 marks*)

e) Compare the reliability of Hall's and Shakespeare's accounts and O'Neil's painting as evidence relating to the events of 1529. (*10 marks*)

3 The Royal Supremacy and the Break with Rome

POINTS TO CONSIDER

This chapter contains a lot of information it is important for you to understand and remember. As you read it for the first time concentrate on establishing the pattern of events in your mind. By the time you finish you should be able to write a few sentences about each of the events included in the list of Key Dates below.

KEY DATES

1529–36	Reformation Parliament
1530	Church charged with praemunire
1531	Charge of praemunire withdrawn in return for a grant of £100,000
1532	Emergence of Thomas Cromwell as the king's chief minister; Supplication against the Ordinaries; Submission of the Clergy; Act in Restraint of Annates
1533	Act in Restraint of Appeals
1534	Act of First Fruits and Tenths; Act of Supremacy; Treasons Act; execution of the Holy Maid of Kent
1534–7	Attack on the Observant Franciscans and the Carthusians
1535	Execution of John Fisher and Sir Thomas More
1536	Act extinguishing the authority of the Bishop of Rome

At the same time the Divorce was being pursued with great energy, several other closely related lines of policy emerged as being of growing importance. The least revolutionary of these was a policy of attacking the Church for its supposed abuses, especially the high fees clergy often charged for their services, and the fact that many senior churchmen held a number of positions simultaneously (a situation known as pluralism) which meant that they could not live in all the places where their duties were supposed to be carried out (known as non-residence). Others advocated going further than reforming the Church. They wanted to reduce its power and independence. Some suggested that this would best be achieved by placing it clearly under the authority of the Crown. There was much discussion of the concept of 'imperium', the idea that England was a fully sovereign and independent entity in which no person and no institution should owe an allegiance to foreigners (such as the Pope). Many of these ideas had to do with putting pressure on Clement VII to rule in Henry's favour by threatening him with what might happen if he did not. Some of the ideas were concerned with finding alternative ways of freeing the king from his wife. However, it appears that they increasingly became viewed in government circles as being desirable ends in themselves. Some historians have been sufficiently confident of this to claim that Henry and his ministers would have acted in the same way, even had Anne Boleyn not been a factor in the equation. They have also claimed that the Reformation would have happened when it did even if the Divorce had not been an issue. But this is not a very convincing argument.

This diversity of aims first became apparent at about the time of Wolsey's fall from power in 1529. It has proved impossible to specify the stages by which the additional policy objectives were adopted, (relevant written evidence probably never existed), but a number of common features have been identified in each case. It is clear that Henry was introduced to a wide range of alternative possible strategies by people who were at the edge of, or even completely outside, government circles. Certainly none of the ideas originated with the aristocratic leaders such as Norfolk, Suffolk or Wiltshire.

It is also clear that the king did not adopt any of the suggestions made to him in their entirety, even though some of them were presented in a fully developed form with detailed proposals about each of the steps to be taken. His approach was to seize upon one element of the policy, normally with great enthusiasm, and to pursue it with vigour for a short time before seemingly losing all interest in it. Some time later he would do the same with a different idea. The result was progress by a sequence of fits and starts, with inconsistencies and contradictions abounding, and short-term goals being the norm.

However, there was no general chaos. Since, in the 1950s, Elton originally developed his theories on the central role played by Thomas Cromwell in the politics of the 1530s, there has been general agreement that some semblance of order and consistency (at least from 1532 onwards) was provided by the activities of the king's unofficial chief minister. Although few writers have been as convinced as Elton that Cromwell had a fully developed vision of the state he wished to create, most historians have recognised that he was the man whose administrative skill and political flexibility ensured that a coherent pattern emerged from what was essentially a sequence of impulsive and insufficiently thought-through royal decisions. The contrast between the conduct of affairs before and after Cromwell's emergence as the king's leading 'man of business' in 1532 would seem to add considerable weight to this interpretation.

1 The Reformation Parliament, 1529–36

> **KEY ISSUE** What was the Reformation Parliament? Why is it thought to have been important?

A parliament was summoned to meet in the autumn of 1529 for the first time in six years. There is no direct evidence to suggest why Henry decided on this course of action. However, it has been claimed that the most likely reasons were that he either intended to use parliament to bring about the fall of Cardinal Wolsey or to increase the pressure on the Pope by demonstrating that the 'political nation' was behind him. Neither of these explanations is very convincing. A more plausible argument is that he had an ill-thought out plan to use parliament to declare his marriage with Catherine of Aragon invalid. However, it is very unlikely that evidence will ever be found to explain why the action was taken. What is clear is that by the time parliament met Henry had given up whatever his plan might have been, and the session was allowed to proceed in a generally aimless fashion until the approach of Christmas gave reason for activity to be suspended until some unspecified time in the future.

Thus began what has been described as being the most important parliament in the nation's history. Certainly the Reformation Parliament (so named in the nineteenth century) played a central role in the revolutionary events that took place during its lifetime, although its meetings were suspended (in technical terms, it was 'prorogued') for much longer than it was in session (it met for only 484 days in seven sessions over six and a half years), and despite the fact that during the time when Henry VIII was taking the policy initiatives it achieved very little of lasting importance. But during the sessions of 1533, 1534 and 1536, when Cromwell was very influential, legislation was enacted which was of very considerable short- and long-term significance. So, from what appears to have been an abortive initial policy decision, a strategy developed that was to become (in Elton's view at least) the central plank in a revolution in government.

2 The Attack on the Church, 1529–34

> **KEY ISSUES** What were the main stages of Henry's attack on the Church? What are the main areas of historical uncertainty?

A second line of policy was also begun in 1529. It was pursued intermittently and with short-term objectives during the next two years, and was finally pushed to its logical conclusion under Cromwell's tutelage. It was the attack on the powers of the Church within Henry's domains.

The first stage occurred almost by chance. During the first session of the Reformation Parliament a small group of MPs, mainly London merchants and lawyers, launched a pre-planned attack on abuses they claimed were widespread within the Church. Most of the evidence about this comes from the well-known Chronicle of Edward Hall, who was probably one of their number. Hall gives the impression that a wave of indignation swept the Commons over the issue, resulting in demands for major legislation to control the way in which churchmen acted. Although for centuries historians took Hall at face value, it is now generally agreed that he greatly exaggerated both the anger and the actions taken by MPs. Certainly the only concrete outcome of this supposed tide of anticlerical sentiment was the passage of three relatively insignificant bills attempting to limit pluralism and non-residence. It has been claimed that Henry allowed this very public attack on the Church to take place because he was pleased to be able to suggest to the Pope that the country was in a state of fervent anticlericalism which could only be controlled by a monarch who had been granted the annulment of his marriage. However, if Hall's account of what happened is somewhat fanciful, this episode must have been rather less significant than it has traditionally been presented as being. Nevertheless, it was noticeable that the king did not instruct those who managed the Commons on his behalf to damp down whatever strength of feeling existed and that he did allow the three anticlerical bills to become law.

It cannot be known how far this episode encouraged Henry to undertake a more general attack on the Church's position. However, what little evidence there is suggests that it was those who 'had his ear' who egged him into taking action. During 1530 there seem to have been three lines of policy being advocated by such people: the weakening of the Church's will to resist whatever the king demanded by taking legal action against either a group of its leading members or churchmen in general; the forcing of the Church to grant the Crown a large sum of money; and the taking of legal control of the Church. In the end a strategy incorporating all three approaches was adopted, although it was clearly the money which interested Henry most. Towards the end of the year the churchmen of England and Wales as a whole were indicted on a charge of praemunire. This was a catch-all legal provision, arising from three fourteenth-century acts of parliament, which forbade clerics to take any action which cut across the powers of the Crown – especially recognising any external authority without the monarch's explicit permission. The law was so phrased that it was virtually impossible for any churchman to carry out his duties without infringing the terms of the act. It was this law that had been used to topple Wolsey and it was now to be used to cow his former colleagues. The charge was that by recognising Wolsey's legatine powers without Henry's permission all churchmen had transgressed the law and were therefore liable to suffer the penalty of surrendering all their property to the Crown.

When the Southern Convocation – the parliament of the Church in England and Wales, except the three northern dioceses of York, Durham and Carlisle – met in January 1531, its members were told that Henry would withdraw the praemunire charge in return for a grant of £100,000 and the awarding to him of the title of 'Supreme Head of the Church in England and Wales'. With the knowledge of what had happened to Wolsey little more than a year before fresh in their memories, the members of convocation (bishops, abbots, and other high-ranking clergy) were in no doubt that the king's intentions were serious. There was therefore little room for manoeuvre and, in the circumstances, they did well to negotiate some significant conces-sions. They could not achieve a reduction in the sum to be paid but they did extract an agreement that it would be paid over a five-year period rather than immediately as originally demanded. In addition, a qualifying clause – 'as far as the word of God allows' – was added to the king's new title. This made it possible for each person to decide for himself what (if anything) Henry's new honour meant in practice. Traditionally it has been assumed that this change was made at Convocation's request and was therefore a sign that the clergy were willing and able to mount a stout defence of their position. However, this assumption has recently been thrown into serious doubt as it appears that the additional wording may have been proposed by Henry's advisers in order to make the total package less obnoxious to the conservative majority within Convocation. But, whatever is the truth of the matter, the whole affair was a resounding success for the Crown and demonstrated that little effective opposition was likely to be mounted when, and if, further demands were made. The fact that Henry seemed to lose interest in the issue once an agreement over money had been struck did not lessen the understanding that his advisers had gained of the Church's vulnerability in dealing with the Crown, despite Convocation's attempt to suggest that their 'generos-ity' was of their own volition and a reward to Henry for the way in which he had protected the Church's interests. The preamble to their grant of £100,000 contained the justification that:

1 for like as he these other days, most studiously with his pen, and most
   sumptuously in battle, defended the universal church (whose humble
   members we be) against enemies ... so also at this present, many our
   enemies, especially the Lutherans, conspiring the mischief and destruc-
5 tion of the church and clergy of England (whose protector and highest
   head he is), and of late raging against the same and personages of the
   prelates of the clergy with their famous lies and cursed books and
   works everywhere dispersed to the intent to blemish and hurt the estimation of the said prelates and clergy and to bring them into common
10 hatred and contempt: his most wise and excellent majesty ... hath [so]
   confounded and repressed them, that now their presumptuous boldness beginneth to rebate.

Constitutional historians have thought it significant that it was decided to confirm both the pardon of the clergy and the terms on which it was granted in an act of parliament. Where the suggestion came from is not known, but it was certainly agreed to by Henry.

A year later the really telling blows were struck. The episode began in early 1532 when the House of Commons petitioned the king to take action against the way in which churchmen abused their legal powers. The petition is known as the Supplication against the Ordinaries – 'ordinaries' was another word for bishops. Historians have continued to disagree over how the Supplication came into existence. Some argue that it arose spontaneously while others maintain that it was engineered in detail by Thomas Cromwell. But there is no dispute over the use Henry made of the document once it came into his hands. He pretended to be the impartial judge in a dispute between two groups of his subjects and passed the petition to Convocation, requesting their response so that he could be informed of the Church's side of the argument before he decided what to do. When he received the churchmen's reply he summoned a deputation of MPs to attend on him and handed a copy of Convocation's defence to them. As he did so he is reported to have said:

> We think their answer will smally please you, for it seemeth to us very slender. You be a great sort of wise men; I doubt not that you will look circumspectly on the matter, and we will be indifferent between you.

But parliament was given no time to act on Henry's broad hint. Almost immediately Convocation was presented with a series of demands by the king. They were to surrender the right to enact new ordinances on their own authority – all future changes in canon law (the legal system followed in church courts) would require the monarch's consent. Existing canon law was to be scrutinised by a committee of 32, half clergy and half laymen, but all appointed by the king, and only those ordinances approved by the committee were to remain in force. This body of law was to stand entirely on the Crown's authority. Thus the intention was that the Church's legal system was to lose its centuries-old independence by being made directly responsible to the king.

Not surprisingly, the members of Convocation were thrown off balance by this bombshell. Most of them seem to have felt instinctively that they must resist this attempt to destroy the Church's legal status as an institution that was parallel to, but separate from, the State. But they were somewhat at a loss in deciding how this could be done. Their leader, William Warham, the aged Archbishop of Canterbury, showed some willingness to fight (possibly because he recognised the approach of death) but he lacked both stamina and a strategy and was soon reduced to virtual impotence by being informed that his monarch was displeased with him. Similar action was used to 'warn off' most other potential opponents, while in a very public display a thinly veiled general threat was issued. Henry summoned a further deputation of MPs to appear before him and pretended to them that he had recently been shown the wording of the two oaths – one to the monarch and one to the Pope – sworn by senior churchmen on taking up a new post. As he handed them copies of the oaths he is reported to have said:

1 Well-beloved subjects, we thought that the clergy of our realm had been our subjects wholly, but now we have well perceived that they be but half our subjects; yea, and scarce our subjects; for all the prelates at their consecration make an oath to the Pope, clean contrary to the
5 oath they make to us, so that they seem to be his subjects, and not ours.

Were the leading members of Convocation meant to conclude that charges of treason might be in the offing unless the king was given what he wanted? If they were, it was an unnecessary use of such 'big guns' because the clergy's will to resist had already been broken. When the king instructed Convocation to make its decision within 24 hours there was a complete capitulation and a document, the Submission of the Clergy, accepting all that was demanded was voted through without opposition. The fact that a large majority of the members of Convocation chose to disassociate themselves from the Submission by being absent from the session at which the vote was taken, so that a minimal number of individuals is recorded as being in favour of the surrender, was of no concern to Henry. He had secured the power he desired. That this was an end in itself, rather than a means to an end, became clear when no action was taken to set up the committee to examine the canon law which Convocation had been forced to accept in their Submission. However, the terms of the surrender were once again confirmed in an act of parliament.

The Church was now virtually powerless to resist further attacks on its position, especially if they were supported by parliament. In 1534 the Act of First Fruits and Tenths established a permanent system of high taxation for the clergy – as opposed to the 'one-off' arrangement of 1531. In future all clerical office holders were to pay the Crown approximately a year's income on appointment (the first fruits) and ten per cent of their income annually thereafter. This system increased the royal revenue by about 40 per cent and was punitive in that laymen were not subjected to taxation on anything like the same scale. The attacks reached their climax when, between 1536 and 1540 (see chapter 4), the majority of the Church's capital assets were confiscated.

3 The Break with Rome

KEY ISSUES What part did Henry VIII play in bringing about the Break with Rome? What part was played by others, especially Thomas Cromwell and Archbishop Cranmer?

At the same time Henry was increasing his control over the Church in England and Wales, he was also taking steps to reduce the power of the Pope within his domains. His motives for doing so were mixed and often confused. For much of the time his intention appears to have been to exert pressure on Rome in the hope of persuading the Pope to reach a favourable decision over the divorce. However, intermittently to begin with, although more consistently as the years passed, there was a second strand to the policy. Henry was periodically convinced – although he frequently lost sight of his conviction – that his aim should be to re-establish his territories as a 'sovereign empire' within which no other ruler could exercise control of any sort. Much of the force of the argument underpinning this policy lay in the word 're-establish'. Those who urged the king in this direction believed that the rulers of England had enjoyed sole power in their kingdoms until some time in the early middle ages when the Pope (unjustifiably in their opinion) had established a variety of legal and financial claims because of his headship of the Western Church. These, it was argued, were all spurious and should be rejected out of hand.

Henry was frequently undecided whether the actions he took against papal power in England were bargaining counters, liable to be reversed if he was granted his divorce, or permanent steps towards a total destruction of foreign influence in his lands. Because of this, it is impossible to be certain of the significance of much of what happened. However, some aspects of the situation are clear. Although the king undoubtedly retained the final say in what happened and was even personally responsible for some of the initiatives that were taken, his vacillations and lack of clarity of purpose were minimised by the consistent sense of direction displayed by a number of his advisers and men of business. This collection of ministers, junior office holders and advisers was able to ensure that consistency finally prevailed and that a complete break with Rome was achieved. Their success, of course, was only possible because the Pope was unprepared to bow to any threat, thus enabling Henry to be persuaded that it was only by throwing off allegiance to Rome that his divorce could be achieved. Once it had been accepted by the king that there could be no going back, the task of those who wished to see an end to papal power in England for reasons unconnected to Anne Boleyn became much more straightforward.

Between the early 1950s and the mid-1970s G.R. Elton established a new orthodoxy to replace the traditional view that the break with Rome occurred because it was the only way in which Henry could free himself from Catherine of Aragon. The basic Elton view was that it was brought about mainly due to Thomas Cromwell, for whom it was a vital stage in the development of the sovereign nation state which he aspired to create. Thus, it has become commonplace to suggest that the divorce was the occasion rather than the cause of the ending of papal power in England, and that (by implication at least) it would

have happened at about the same time whether or not Henry had had
marital problems to resolve. Although Elton has modified and quali-
fied his views over the years and other historians have chosen to slant
their accounts of events slightly differently, the essentials of the Elton
orthodoxy remain intact. As a result, the false starts and changes of
direction caused by Henry's confusions are thought of as being less
significant than they once were.

One important qualification that has been generally accepted
since Elton first presented his interpretation is that Cromwell was not
the initiator, or at times, even the prime mover of the policy that is so
closely associated with his name. Two other men in particular are
judged to have played an important role in these events, although it
has never been suggested that they should be regarded as challenging
Cromwell's claim to be the pre-eminent influence. Thomas Cranmer
rose to real prominence in 1532 when he was chosen as Archbishop
of Canterbury. But even before then he had argued strongly that the
king should be the head of all institutions within his realm, including
the Church. His reasoning was that God had always intended the
rulers he placed in power to have such all-embracing authority and
that it was only the usurpations of the popes which had interfered
with this divinely ordained system of government. His aim was to see
the clock turned back to the time when, he claimed, the situation had
been as God intended. Christopher St German had for many years
been the country's leading theorist about the law and, in particular,
about the system of common law. Although he was a very old man for
the time (he was in his seventies) when the question of papal influence in England came to be of interest in the highest political circles,
he still possessed the energy and the clarity of mind to produce
detailed theoretical justifications for the elimination of the Pope's
authority outside of Rome.

The body of ideas put forward by Cranmer and St German is given
the name of 'caesaro-papism'. This is because it was advocated that
the same person be both the temporal leader (Caesar, as in the
Roman Empire) and the religious leader (the Pope). It is not surprising that Henry, given his enormous ego, should be attracted to such
thinking. In 1530 he instructed Cranmer, along with another junior
colleague, to gather together all the historical evidence they could to
support their case. The result was a handwritten collection of documents known as the *collectanea satis copiosa*. Although it included many
items that were (unknown to Cranmer) medieval forgeries, its contents were taken at their face value and were much used to justify the
king's case in the years to come. Typical of such documents was a
letter supposed to have been written by a second-century pope to a
king of Britain. It read:

> You seek from us the Roman and imperial laws to be sent to you, which
> you wish to use in the kingdom of Britain. The Roman and imperial laws
> you may always reprove, but the law of God we may not. You have

received recently by divine mercy the law and faith of Christ in the king-
5 dom of Britain. You have with you in the kingdom both books of scripture, from which by God's grace with the counsel of your realm take a
law, and by that law through God's sufferance rule your kingdom of
Britain. For you are vicar of God in your kingdom . . . The omnipotent
God grant you so to rule the kingdom of Britain that you may reign with
10 him eternally, whose vicar you are in the said realm.

Could there be clearer evidence than this that the Pope should hold
no power in England?

However, it was not until Cromwell became the major influence on
Henry, at some time in 1532, that the decision was reached to break
completely with Rome. The new chief minister probably used the twin
arguments that this was the only way of being sure that the divorce
would be granted and that the king owed it to himself and his successors to regain the powers that had been stolen from his ancestors
by fraudulent means. Thus the two strands of policy in dealing with
the Pope were brought together – at least, as far as the king's stated
intentions were concerned. But Cromwell must have been made very
anxious at times over the next year or two when it became apparent
that, in his heart of hearts, his master still harboured hopes of reaching some agreement with Rome. Fortunately for Cromwell's plans
(and probably for his continued physical well-being), a mixture of
papal intransigence and English diplomatic clumsiness meant that
nothing resulted from Henry's further attempts to reach an agreed
solution in his 'great matter'. Possibly this was Cromwell's first experience of coping with a monarch who was able simultaneously to hold
and to act on diametrically opposite views, ideas and policies.

The first official step taken to lessen the Pope's influence in
England was the passage of the Act in Restraint of Annates in 1532,
which banned the payment of all but five per cent of annates. Annates
were moneys equivalent to about one-third of their annual income
paid to the Pope by all new holders of senior posts within the Church
in England and Wales and were the papacy's main source of income
from Henry's kingdom. The fact that the act was conditional – it did
not come into effect until the king issued letters patent to activate it
– confirms that the measure was part of the programme aimed at
making it worth the Pope's while to grant Henry the divorce he
sought. Even the provision in the act to remove from the Pope and to
give to the king the power to give final confirmation to all senior clerical posts was probably merely intended to deny the Pope an obvious
tit-for-tat response.

The really important policy decision was made later in the year at
a time when Cromwell's influence was effectively undisputed. The
plan was to end the Papacy's right to act as the final court of appeal
in most matters governed by canon law, and to legislate that the
majority of most legal rulings (including those to do with marriage)
were to be made within England. The short-term effect of this was, of

course, to ensure that the final verdict on the validity of Henry and Catherine's marriage would be taken out of Rome's hands, but its real significance was that, in order to justify the change, the right of the Pope to make decisions affecting Henry and his subjects had to be denied. It used to be thought that this course of action was only decided on once it was known that Anne Boleyn was pregnant, and that Henry was merely reacting to immediate circumstances in agreeing to this hardening of policy. However, it now seems more likely that Anne Boleyn only began to sleep with her monarch once the policy decision to break decisively with Rome had been made in principle and that the only effect of the pregnancy was to inject a sense of urgency into the work of securing the necessary legislation. In March 1533 the Act in Restraint of Appeals (often referred to simply as the Act of Appeals) passed through both houses of parliament and received the royal assent. Its preamble, which contained the justification for what was being done, argued:

1 Where by divers sundry old authentic histories and chronicles it is man-
   ifestly declared and expressed that this realm of England is an empire,
   and so hath been accepted in the world, governed by one supreme head
   and king having the dignity and royal estate of the imperial crown of the
5 same, unto whom a body politic, compact of all sorts and degrees of
   people divided in terms by names of spirituality and temporality, be
   bounden and owe to bear next to God a natural and humble obedience;
   he [the king] being also institute and furnished by the goodness and sufferance of Almighty God with plenary, whole and entire power, pre-
10 eminence, authority, prerogative, and jurisdiction to render and yield
   justice and final determination to all manner of folk, residents and subjects within the realm, in all causes, matters, debates and contentions
   happening to occur, insurge or begin within the limits thereof, without
   restraint or provocation to any foreign prince or potentates of the
15 world ...

The act went on to stipulate that it was no longer permissible for any of the king's subjects to appeal to an authority outside the country on a specified list of issues and that the Archbishop of Canterbury would henceforth assume the legal powers over these matters that had previously resided in the Pope. Within two months Cranmer had decided, under the terms of the act, that the papal dispensation allowing Henry and Catherine to marry was invalid and that they had therefore never been husband and wife. It seems that Henry might have been prepared to allow matters to rest there, or even to restore the Pope to his previous position had he, despite the lateness of the hour, been willing to give his blessing to the divorce and to Catherine's replacement by Anne Boleyn. But within a year it was clear that no possibility of a rapprochement remained. What had seemed to be a promising diplomatic opening engineered via the King of France had come to nothing and in 1534 Clement VII had finally announced that

SEVENTH BOOK,

Beginning with the Reign of King HENRY the Eighth.

Allegory of the Reformation from John Foxe's Book of Martyrs, a massively influential piece of Protestant propaganda published during the reign of Elizabeth I.

Catherine was legally Henry's wife and therefore still the Queen of England. Cromwell was well pleased. He was able to capitalise on his master's fury to obtain permission to complete the work that the Act of Appeals had started and to eliminate every trace of papal power in England.

Between 1534 and 1536 the Reformation Parliament passed a series of acts to ensure that this was done. All direct payments to the Pope were halted (the money went to the king instead), the Archbishop of Canterbury was empowered to grant the wide variety of dispensations and personal exemptions that had previously only been available from Rome (this probably damaged the papacy financially much more than the cessation of direct payments), and the Pope's role in the appointment of churchmen and in the definition of beliefs and religious practices was eliminated (these powers now passed to the Crown). The aptly named 'Act extinguishing the authority of the Bishop of Rome' (1536) tied up the loose ends and laid down the loss of all property as the punishment for people who defended any of the Pope's former powers. Within two years anyone who referred to the former head of the Church as other than the Bishop of Rome was likely to be suspected of being a traitor, as were priests who merely covered up rather than crossed out the Pope's name in their service books. Although it was Thomas Cromwell who took anti-papalism to such lengths, he was fully supported by a bitter and vengeful Henry VIII.

4 The Royal Supremacy

> **KEY ISSUES** Did the break with Rome necessarily mean royal supremacy? What arguments have traditionally been made by historians claiming that the break with Rome was very significant? What arguments have been advanced to suggest that the break with Rome was of little political significance?

When the Pope's powers within England were removed, there was no automatic reason why they should have been handed over to the king. There were other options available. There was a large number of people, mainly within the ranks of the clergy, strongly opposed to any layman exercising control over the Church. Although they saw no reason why the present situation should be altered, they might have been prepared to lend their support to an arrangement whereby a Church of England was established which owed no allegiance to any authority outside the kingdom but was independent of the temporal state. But Henry VIII had attacked on the autonomy of the Church in 1531 and 1532. This had shown that such a solution would be unacceptable to him. It is probable that Thomas Cromwell favoured a different option. There is considerable evidence that he wished the Pope's former powers to be vested in the king-in-parliament, rather than reverting to the king alone. It has been suggested that it was because of this ministerial desire to see decisions about the new Church of England taken by a partnership of monarch and parliament on a continuing basis that every stage in the transfer of authority from the Pope was authorised by legislation, rather than resting on the will of the king alone. There has even been a claim (no longer taken seriously) that Cromwell was successful in implementing his policy. However, it is now generally accepted that the king's leading minister failed in his attempt to develop a permanent interdependent relationship between the monarch and the political nation (as represented by parliament). Henry was determined that his authority should remain unrestricted by any such arrangement. His interest was in removing any constraints on his freedom of action rather than in establishing a constitutional partnership with his subjects. As far as he was concerned, the Crown was the only acceptable place for the ex-papal powers to reside.

This was made very clear by the wording of the Act of Supremacy of 1534 in which the king's supreme headship of the Church was not granted but was recognised as an existing fact. Thus parliament was not giving powers to the Crown (if it had been, it might later have decided to withdraw them). It was merely confirming the situation and defining in legal terms what was assumed to be a God-given authority The full title of the act carries something of the flavour of what was intended. It was 'an act concerning the King's Highness to be Supreme Head of the Church of England and to have authority to reform and redress all errors, heresies and abuses in the same'. A similar message was contained in the act's opening sentences:

1 Albeit the King's Majesty justly and rightfully is and oweth to be the supreme head of the Church of England, and so is recognised by the clergy of this realm in their Convocations; yet nevertheless for corroboration and confirmation thereof, and for the increase of virtue in
5 Christ's religion within the realm of England, and to repress and extirp all errors heresies and other enormities and abuses heretofore used in the same, be it enacted by authority of this present parliament that the king our sovereign lord, his heirs and successors kings of this realm, shall be taken, accepted and reputed the only supreme head in earth of
10 the Church of England called Anglicana Ecclesia ...

Gone was the qualification of the supreme headship to which Convocation had agreed in 1531 (see page 38) and gone was any implication that this was largely an honorific title. It was now made plain that the Church was to be subjected to lay control in matters of its day-to-day management and was not to be left in control of its own affairs, as many clerics had mistakenly assumed that it would be. Before the end of the year Cromwell was appointed as the king's vicegerent in spiritual matters. This meant that, as far as the Church was concerned, he was in a position to exercise all the powers that legally belonged to the king. And he was not slow to make full use of his new authority (see pages 65 and 102), so that bishops and other senior churchmen soon found their work being closely scrutinised and themselves subjected to a steady stream of detailed written instructions about what should and should not be done.

It has often been argued that the coming of the royal supremacy over the Church constituted a revolutionary change in the English constitution. How justified is this claim? In many respects the case has been overstated. It has been customary to contrast a state in which an institution (the Church) with its independent legal system and owning about one third of the country's landed property was controlled by a foreign power – the pre-Reformation situation – with a modern nation state in which all final authority resided in the monarch – the post-Reformation situation. However, the difference was not as great as it might seem when described in this way. The difficulty is in the word 'controlled', which undoubtedly gives an inflated impression of the influence that the Papacy exercised over the English Church in the decades before the 1530s. If one discounts the way in which Wolsey used his position as papal legate to establish a virtual dictatorship over his colleagues at all levels (as it seems reasonable to do as Wolsey was hardly a 'foreign power'), it is clear that the Pope played very little part in ecclesiastical affairs on the English side of the cliffs of Dover. Although his was the final decision in the appointment to senior positions such as bishoprics, there was a long-established tradition that he invariably confirmed the person nominated by the king. Rome was rarely appealed to in cases of canon law, and when it was it was always by the tiny minority of the population which was in a position to pay the high fees (in practice, bribes) required to achieve a successful outcome in the Roman courts. Thus the effect of the appeal system on the English Church as a whole was minimal – although it could be devastating on individuals, as Henry VIII found to his cost. Nor did the Pope tell English Christians what to believe. The basic teachings of the Church were so well established and unchanging that they required no definition from the centre, and the time had not arrived when it was felt necessary to make rulings on matters of detail. It was left to theologians, mainly studying in universities, to debate the finer points of dogma among themselves and to agree or disagree as they chose. It was only during the period of the 'official' Counter-Reformation, after the death of Henry VIII, that Rome felt the need to act as the arbiter on matters of belief and religious practice. Some of the legislation passed by the Reformation Parliament referred to the large sums of money that the Pope gained from England because of his 'usurpation'. However, these complaints were made largely for propaganda purposes and had little substance in fact. While it is true that the Papacy drained huge amounts of gold and silver from Germany, as was so vociferously complained of by Luther and others, the same was not the case with England where the 'exactions' were hardly noticeable. The only general levy was one of several centuries' standing – Peter's Pence – and it raised no more than a few hundred pounds per year from the country as a whole!

If the case for a dramatic extinction of foreign influence within the English state is less than totally convincing, what of the claim that the royal supremacy radically altered the constitution itself? Even here the traditional interpretation appears to be somewhat overstated. The picture has frequently been painted of the pre-Reformation Church forming a state within a state and therefore preventing the development of 'modern' political institutions. Two aspects of the Church's legal independence – benefit of clergy and sanctuaries – have normally been described as typifying this situation. Benefit of clergy was the arrangement whereby any person charged in one of the king's courts could claim to be immune from prosecution if he was in holy orders. As all those who played some official part, however minor, in Church life and not just priests were considered to be in holy orders, and as, in the absence of documentation to prove a person's status, those who claimed benefit of clergy had only to be able to read a verse of Latin to escape the clutches of the law, there was an obvious loophole for educated (or even intelligent) rogues to exploit. Sanctuaries were areas of land, ranging in size from the county of Durham to the environs of particular churches or monasteries, which were outside the jurisdiction of the law of the land. People whose normal place of residence was within a sanctuary could claim to be exempt from the normal processes of the law wherever the crime of which they were charged had been committed. Many historians have stated (or at least implied) that while such anomalies existed it would have been impossible for a fully-fledged nation state to have developed, and that the royal supremacy, by bringing the Church's legal system under the Crown's control, removed a bar to important constitutional developments.

However, it is doubtful whether the bar was of great significance in reality. Not only had the numbers of people abusing the Church's legal privileges always been small, but legislation in the early Tudor period had also lessened the problem by removing some exemptions entirely – especially for major crimes such as murder and high treason – and by ensuring that those that remained were claimed only once by any individual (claimants were branded on the thumb to prevent them using the same 'escape' a second time). The net result was that the existence of the clerical legal privileges has been assessed as being no more than a minor inconvenience, and certainly not one which would have seriously inhibited the emergence of England as a unitary nation state.

So was the royal supremacy of any great significance? It seems that it was because, with hindsight, historians have been able to detect that it marked a dramatic shift in the balance of power within the state. By the 1530s the secular arm was definitely the dominant partner. This was most graphically exemplified by the fact that, although the southern Convocation was always summoned to meet at the same time as parliament, it was normally a largely irrelevant side-show. However, it is clear that the Church was still a major force in the land. But it rapidly declined in both political and constitutional importance after 1534. Church courts continued in existence but they no longer offered any challenge to their civil counterparts, and churchmen largely ceased to play a prominent part in political affairs. With the brief exception of Stephen Gardiner during Queen Mary's reign, Wolsey was the last in a long line of clerical Lord Chancellors. And, after 1540, with the final disappearance of the monasteries (see page 69), laymen secured a large majority in the House of Lords. Never again would it be possible to think of the Church as providing a potential alternative power base to the monarchy within the state. Yet even this judgement should perhaps be treated with caution, for there are some commentators who have credibly maintained that the royal supremacy was no more than a symbol of changes that were going to happen in any case, whether or not there had been a break with Rome. Although by their very nature hypothetical arguments can never be proved or disproved, it does seem likely that a mid-sixteenth century English state remaining within the Roman Catholic fold would have reached an agreement with the Papacy which would have had much the same effect as the legislation of 1534–6. At least, such would have been the case were English monarchs to have acted in much the same way as their powerful continental counterparts had done. Thus, as is explored in chapter 5, the real significance of the royal supremacy and the break with Rome may in fact have been religious rather than political.

5 Opposition to the Changes

> **KEY ISSUE** What methods did Henry and Cromwell use to overcome opposition to the new order of things?

a) The Government's Strategy

Both Henry VIII and Thomas Cromwell realised that the policies they were pursuing after 1532 were going to be unpopular in many quarters and were likely to be actively supported by very few people. Therefore they consciously developed an approach for dealing with what could have been a very perilous situation indeed. Working from indirect evidence it is possible to identify this approach with confidence. The potential opposition was seemingly divided into two categories – those (a tiny minority) who would refuse to accept the changes whatever was done to them, and those (the large majority) who would fall into line provided the stakes were raised high enough. Given this analysis, the strategy to be followed was clear. The small number of unyielding opponents must be destroyed, partly to act as a warning to others, and the mass of less determined doubters must be forced into positive acceptance of the new situation by threatening them with dire consequences if they did not.

Cromwell believed very strongly that all such action must be legally defensible and it appears that the king agreed with him. So it was necessary to ensure that appropriate legislation was in place to justify whatever action was taken. The traditional way of dealing with traitors, especially where the evidence against them was not clear-cut (as was often the case), was for parliament to pass an act of attainder against them. Such acts were normally passed without there being a trial – a statement by a minister claiming guilt was usually sufficient – and condemned the alleged traitors to death and transferred their property to the Crown. Although such a procedure could be used if necessary, it was clear to Cromwell that it would be a clumsy method of dealing with a number of cases arising over an extended period of time. What was needed was a blanket law which could be invoked as and when the need arose. This was provided by a Treasons Act, originally passed in 1534 and strengthened by amendment on several occasions in the following years. The act specified that any person was guilty of high treason (punishable by death) who

1 do maliciously wish, will or desire by words or writing, or by craft imagine, invent, practise, or attempt any bodily harm to be done or committed to the king's most royal person, the queen's [Anne Boleyn] or their heir's apparent [Elizabeth], or to deprive them of any of their
5 dignity, title or name of their royal estates, or slanderously and maliciously publish and pronounce, by express writing or words, that the king should be heretic, schismatic, tyrant, infidel or usurper of the crown . . .

The initial draft of the law had worried many MPs, especially in that it laid open to prosecution anybody who made a hostile comment about the king, possibly in a moment of anger. In order to allay such concerns the word 'maliciously' (implying evil intent) was added in several places. Even so, the act made any expression of dissent about what the king had done (be it the divorce, the break with Rome or the royal supremacy) highly dangerous. In such circumstances a prudent person would be unwise to engage in any discussion of what had happened, especially when life imprisonment was later established as the punishment for anyone who heard treasonable utterances and failed to report them.

Cromwell was rightly confident that everybody who spoke out would be able to be dealt with under such legislation. But silence was not to be allowed to protect the passive majority of dissidents. Within the legislation confirming the break with Rome, the royal supremacy and the new order of succession following the divorce (Anne Boleyn's children to have precedence and Catherine of Aragon's daughter, Mary, to be disinherited), clauses were inserted requiring the entire population, as required, to swear oaths supporting the new arrangements. Death was to be the punishment for those who refused. It was felt in government circles that a sufficient deterrent was in place.

b) The Holy Maid of Kent

However, even before these arrangements were made one or two highly publicised centres of opposition had emerged. The most dangerous of these revolved around the person of Elizabeth Barton, known as the Holy Maid of Kent. Since the mid-1520s she had claimed to have a series of visions during which the Virgin Mary, in particular, spoke to her and gave her instructions to pass on to others. In the south-east of England (she was a nun in Canterbury) she enjoyed a widespread reputation among both the rich and the poor as God's mouthpiece and it was said that many of the most powerful people in the land were afraid of her. From the outset she had spoken out against the king's attempts to have his marriage annulled. She had even told Henry to his face that he would be punished by God if he continued with his efforts. When the divorce was announced in May 1533 she very publicly prophesied that within a month Henry would cease to be king – leaving those who heard of her words to decide for themselves whether it would be because God was about to strike him down or because his subjects were about to overthrow him. Such a situation called for swift and decisive action if the danger of widespread public disturbances was to be avoided. The Maid was immediately arrested, brought to London, and forced (with a handful of her leading supporters) to announce at St Paul's Cross that all her visions were fraudulent and a hoax. She and five of her closest associates were then imprisoned in the Tower, an act of attainder was passed against them when parliament met in early 1534 and in April they were executed. One crisis had been averted.

c) The Observant Franciscans and the Carthusians

Less alarming, but still highly irritating to the king, were the criticisms of his treatment of Catherine and of the Pope made by numbers of monks and friars who were closely associated with the Court. What was particularly galling was that they belonged to the two religious orders – the Observant Franciscan friars and the Carthusian monks – which were generally thought to be the most spiritually admirable in the country. In addition, they were geographically well situated to provide hope and encouragement to anyone else who wished to stand up to Henry. The main Franciscan friary was alongside the king's most frequented palace at Greenwich, and the Carthusians' most important centre was the Charterhouse in London. Both were regularly visited by many of the leading figures in society, who were keen to be seen to be associated with such obvious purity of religion.

Investigations soon revealed that the Observant friars were united in their opposition to Henry's policies. Therefore the only action open to the government was to close all seven of their houses nationwide and to force their former inmates out of public view. This was done in 1534 and the more stubborn members were imprisoned. It is not clear what happened to them but the probability is that up to 30 of the 200 Observants died in unnoticed captivity.

However, there seemed to be a possibility of 'dividing and ruling' with the Carthusians. This was because there were some individuals within the London Charterhouse, and many more in the houses in the provinces, who were critical of the uncompromising stance taken by their colleagues. Cromwell hoped to achieve a propaganda victory by showing that the Carthusians had been brought to see reason. But just the opposite occurred. As the leading intransigents were removed to be sent elsewhere, to be imprisoned or even to be executed, a new crop of potential martyrs emerged to carry on the resistance. Over a period of three years 18 members of the Charterhouse were either executed or were starved to death (rather than submission) in prison. In the process a series of stories of outstanding courage were enacted which has been retold to great effect by Catholic writers over the centuries. In the end the king won a hollow victory when a rump of Carthusians swore the oaths which were demanded of them, and the monastery continued a truncated existence until 1539. But the verdict of History has not been kind and the war of attrition against the London Carthusians has often been judged to be one of Henry VIII's least defensible actions.

d) John Fisher

However, contemporaries were more critical of the way in which two prominent individuals – John Fisher and Sir Thomas More – were treated. Fisher was the one member of the Church hierarchy to remain unwavering in his opposition to what Henry was doing. His position was simple and straightforward. He believed that the powers claimed by the Papacy were genuine and God-given, that anybody who denied them was committing a mortal sin and that it was the duty of the Church to denounce such action. He was so certain of his beliefs that he was prepared to stand by them whatever the cost to himself or to anybody else. There was no room for compromise in this stance.

By the time the breach with Rome occurred Fisher was an old man in his mid-sixties. He had been the Bishop of Rochester in Kent since 1504, and the fact that he had never been promoted from this the smallest and poorest diocese in England suggests much about him. He was a very untypical bishop in that he had no worldly ambition, was unskilled in politics and showed few administrative capabilities. His loves were scholarship (he learned Hebrew in his fifties) and prayer (to which he devoted many hours every day). He only became a bishop because it was the wish of Henry VIII's mother, whose spiritual adviser he was, that he do so.

He came to Henry VIII's notice as the most active of Catherine of Aragon's defenders during the struggle over the divorce (see page 12). His outspokenness, both to the king's face and in print, resulted in him becoming loathed by Henry, who seems to have been determined to punish him for his effrontery when the right opportunity presented itself. This seemed to have come in 1533 because Fisher was a declared supporter of the Holy Maid of Kent. But, for some reason, Henry decided to wait a little longer and, although Fisher was named in the act of attainder passed against Elizabeth Barton and her associates, he was allowed to purchase his freedom by paying a relatively small fine. However, the reprieve was short lived. When, in April 1534, he refused to swear the oath accepting the divorce and all that had flowed from it he was imprisoned in the Tower. The 'politic' thing for Henry to have done would have been to leave him there to die from the harsh conditions in which he was kept. But a year later the king was goaded into giving a public display of his power. The Pope had just announced that Fisher was to be made a cardinal. Henry's response was predictable. The cardinal-to-be was accused of high treason, was tried and executed. Although everything had been done according to the law – Fisher was clearly guilty of the charge against him – there was a widespread feeling that spite was the real reason for what had happened. Certainly Henry had provided further ammunition to those who wished to portray him as a tyrant.

e) Sir Thomas More

Sir Thomas More was one of the most fascinating characters of the early sixteenth century. If writers have found it easy to describe and to agree on the personality and character of John Fisher, as a group they have been perplexed by Thomas More. The result has been that over the centuries there have been almost as many published pages devoted to discussing what sort of man he was as there have been to assessing Henry VIII. And the variety of judgements offered has been almost as large. At one extreme, he has been presented as a flawless saint (he was canonised by the Catholic Church, along with Fisher, in 1935), while his detractors have portrayed him as a confused genius who unnecessarily sacrificed his life for a technicality. So much conflicting evidence exists that there is never likely to be a consensus among historians about him. This leaves plenty of room for you to exercise an independence of judgement.

Sir Thomas More by Hans Holbein.

Edward Hall's description of Sir Thomas More

I cannot tell whether I should call him a foolish wise man or a wise foolish man, for undoubtedly he beside his learning had a great wit, but it was so mingled with taunting and mocking that it seemed to them that best knew him, that he thought nothing to be well spoken except he had ministered some mock in the communication.

However, there is general agreement about the facts of the major events in his life and about many of his dominant attributes and characteristics. He was born in 1478 in London and spent almost his whole life in the city and its environs. He followed his father's footsteps into the law but, although he became expert in it, he was equally interested in all other branches of learning. His intellect and ability to work hard were such that, before the age of 30, he had established a reputation as one of Europe's leading scholars. His well developed social skills (when he chose to use them) made him highly popular in some circles and the young Henry VIII came to regard him as a friend. Not satisfied with a successful legal career and an outstanding academic career, More was prepared to be drawn into the political court circle and to act as the king's representative in a wide variety of diplomatic situations. In the process he became thought of as a very able and totally reliable royal servant. His strict moral code prevented him from doing the things needed to become a front-line political figure and it was therefore something of a surprise when he was chosen to succeed Wolsey as Lord Chancellor in 1529. This was especially so as he was known by Henry VIII and by his leading courtiers to be opposed to the divorce on principle. The new Lord Chancellor set himself the task of eradicating heresy in England, following a long period during which his predecessor had virtually turned a blind eye to its existence. As a result of his initiative numbers of both Lutherans and less radical reformers were burned at the stake. Henry's mounting attack on the independence of the Church (see page 36) led More to feel unbearably uncomfortable remaining in office as here was another matter of principle over which he could not agree with his master. His belief was that the Church would no longer be spoken to directly by God if it fell under lay control. Henry finally allowed him to resign once the Submission of the Clergy had been safely made in 1532.

The two men's perception of their relationship was now radically different. More regarded himself as the king's loyal servant who would always obey his monarch to the very limit his conscience would allow and who would never do anything actively to oppose him. Henry thought of his former Lord Chancellor as a dangerous enemy (anybody who was not for him was against him) who had deserted him in his hour of greatest need and who deserved to be punished for what he had done. The hatred he frequently felt for his erstwhile friend was extreme. The collision course had been set. More tried to retire completely from public life but Henry was determined to corner him. Cromwell would have been satisfied with More's assurance that he would do nothing to aid or assist the king's opponents but his master insisted that the oath, which he knew contained sentiments with which More fundamentally disagreed, must be sworn. More could not be persuaded to do so. He joined Fisher in the Tower, was tried and was found guilty on a legal technicality. He was executed in July 1535, a month after his distinguished co-prisoner. Henry had dealt his own reputation a further unnecessary blow.

6 Why was there so little Opposition to the Royal Supremacy and the Break with Rome?

> **KEY ISSUE** What explanations for the relative lack of opposition to Henry have been given?

Although there was a small amount of well-publicised opposition to Henry's policies, the reaction in the country as a whole was one of passive acceptance. Historians have not been slow to speculate about why this was so.

It used to be assumed by Protestant writers that the seeming indifference among the population as a whole was an indication that Christian commitment was at a very low ebb in England and Wales by 1530. The picture painted was of a Church in crisis which had lost the support of the people and which was vulnerable to the least political pressure. A variation on this basic explanation was that an already parlous situation had been made untenable by the activities of Wolsey who had destroyed any spirit of resistance that might have existed among the Church hierarchy. Either way, the emphasis was placed on the Church's deficiencies, in that it was a fruit ripe for the plucking.

In recent decades the explanation has been sought on the other side of the coin. Attention has been concentrated on the way in which Cromwell, with Henry's active support, made it virtually impossible for concerted opposition to form. The most that could happen was that relatively isolated pockets of dissent could arise, only to be eliminated before they could act as a focus for wider discontent. In poker-playing parlance, the good cards were all in the government's hands and when it was time for the betting to begin the stakes were made so high that only those with a strong self-destructive urge were prepared to challenge the dealer. After all, it has been argued, the fact that few people were prepared to risk death and the ruin of their family for one part of their traditional faith does not mean that their religion meant little to them.

Summary Diagram
The Royal Supremacy and the Break with Rome

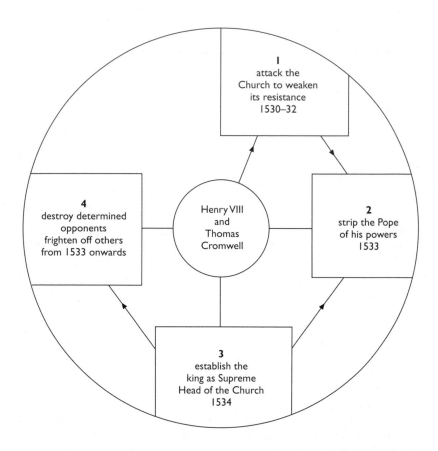

Working on Chapter 3

As the events described and discussed in this chapter form the core of the Henrician Reformation, it is necessary to know as much as you can about them. This suggests that your notes should be full.

You would be well advised to begin by building up a clear picture of what happened and when. The entries in the list of Key Dates at the start of the chapter should provide a suitable framework for this section of your notes.

You then need to make a record of the possible standpoints on the three main historical issues involved: i) why did these events take place?, ii) what was their significance?, and iii) why was there so little opposition to what was done? If you can, you should develop a point of view of your own.

Answering structured and essay questions on Chapter 2

This is a popular topic on which to set structured questions. Examine this structured question:

a) Give an account of Henry VIII's attack on the Church in England between 1529 and 1533. (*10 marks*)
b) Explain why Henry VIII had broken with Rome by 1536. (*10 marks*)
c) How effectively did Henry VIII deal with opposition to his policy? (*5 marks*)

As always, one of the keys to success in answering this three-part question is to identify exactly what you are being asked to do. When answering part a) it is vital to decide on the meaning of the phrase 'give an account of'. Unless you appreciate that what you are being asked to do is to both describe and explain you are very likely to throw away a number of marks, even if you have learned the facts thoroughly. What is the key phrase in part b)? Make sure you understand the difference between 'describe' and 'explain'. Remember that when you explain something it is often helpful to include different points of view, and that you will usually score more highly if you can link each point of view to either a particular historian or a period of historical study.

If you are going to be required to write essays on this topic, study the following questions.

1. Why did Henry VIII break with Rome?
2. How far was the break with Rome caused by political rather than religious factors?
3. Why was there so little effective opposition to Henry VIII's rejection of the Pope and introduction of the royal supremacy?
4. 'Henry VIII was able to dominate the Church in England after 1529 because Cardinal Wolsey had prepared the way for him.' Discuss this verdict.
5. Discuss the role of parliament in the break with Rome and the establishment of the royal supremacy.
6. To what extent was Thomas Cromwell responsible for the lack of active opposition to Henry VIII's assumption of power over the Church?
7. Do you agree with the opinion that 'the beginnings of the Reformation in England owed more to anticlericalism than to Anne Boleyn'?

These questions nearly all focus on one or other of the two aspects of this part of the topic which are most popular among examiners. These might be labelled 'the causes of the Henrician Reformation' and 'the reasons for the lack of opposition to Henry's religious policies'. Clearly, you would be well advised to prepare yourself particularly carefully on both of these issues. If you prepared a list of questions on each issue, into which group would number 4 fit? Which of the seven questions fits into neither group?

A useful starting point when tackling any essay question is to assign it to one of the four standard types of question at this level ('What?', 'Why?', 'How far/To what extent?' and 'challenging statement'). Question 5 is the only one of those listed above that ought to require more than a moment's thought when doing this. Once you have identified a question's type you should be well on the way to deciding your approach to answering it – that is, if you have already developed a strategy for dealing with each type of question. If you have not, perhaps now is the time to talk to somebody about it.

When preparing an essay plan the next task after classifying a question by type is to scrutinise its wording in order to detect any assumptions that will require comment. Most questions contain none, but the procedure is still worth carrying out because it takes only a few seconds and can result in extra marks being gained. Look at question 3. Which of the assumptions being made needs to be dealt with in your answer ('effective' is the clue)? The introductory paragraph of an essay is the obvious place in which to comment on the wording of a question. After all, the purpose of such a paragraph is to capture the reader's attention by showing that you are aware of the significance of the question and by briefly indicating how you intend to deal with it. Drawing attention to assumptions being made by the question is an integral part of this process and can often provide material for a striking first sentence. If you are able to do this it will ensure that your work avoids the fate suffered by many opening paragraphs – being virtually ignored by the examiner because it has no substance, merely being used as a doorway into the essay proper. Writing opening paragraphs that score marks is a skill that is only acquired by thoughtful practice. Attempting to construct a suitable opening to an essay in answer to question 3 could be a useful exercise, especially if you were able to begin by completing a sentence such as, 'What is really surprising about the opposition to the steps taken by Henry VIII between 1533 and 1536 to secure control of the English Church is not that ...'

Source-based questions on Chapter 3

1. Convocation in 1531

Carefully read the extract from Convocation's document on page 38, granting Henry VIII £100,000. Answer the following questions.

a) What impression is Convocation attempting to give about its motives for granting the king so much money? (*2 marks*)

b) What evidence is there that Convocation is attempting to flatter the king? Use quotes from the extract in your answer. (*3 marks*)

c) 'The authors of the document were attempting to influence the king.' Elucidate and justify this statement. (*5 marks*)

d) Why was Convocation unsuccessful in resisting the king's demands in 1531? (*5 marks*)

2. The Submission of the Clergy, 1532
Carefully read the two statements, on pages 39 and 40, reported to have been made by Henry VIII to deputations from the House of Commons in 1532. Answer the following questions.

a) Describe the circumstances in which the two statements were made. (*4 marks*)
b) What were the king's motives in making the statements? (*4 marks*)
c) Both Henry and his audience recognised that some of what he said was either untrue or purposely misleading. However, all concerned understood that this was a normal part of the political 'game'. Identify what was untrue in the first extract and what was misleading in the second. (*4 marks*)
d) It has often been claimed that Henry VIII was very skilful in his handling of parliament. Do these extracts help to substantiate such claims? Explain your answer. (*3 marks*)

3. The Royal Supremacy
Carefully read the extracts from the supposed letter of a second-century pope (page 42), from the preamble to the Act of Appeals of 1533 (page 44), and from the preamble to the Act of Supremacy of 1534 (page 47). Answer the following questions.

a) Explain the implications of the following phrases: i) 'vicar of God' in the first extract, ii) 'this realm of England is an empire' in the second extract, and iii) 'for corroboration and confirmation thereof' in the third extract. (*9 marks*)
b) What internal evidence is there that the first document is a forgery? (*3 marks*)
c) In what ways are the preambles to the two acts purposely misleading? (*4 marks*)
d) What was the function of the preambles of government-inspired acts of parliament in the 1530s? (*4 marks*)

4. The Treasons Act, 1534
Carefully read the extract from the Treasons Act of 1534 given on page 51. Answer the following questions.

a) Explain 'by craft imagine, invent, practise, or attempt' (line 1). (*2 marks*)
b) In what way was the wording of the legislation changed between the time it was introduced to parliament and the time it became law? Why was this change made? (*3 marks*)
c) What three main types of action did the act outlaw? (*3 marks*)
d) What major criticism of the act has been made by twentieth-century commentators? (*2 marks*)

5. Sir Thomas More

Study the portrait of Sir Thomas More and carefully read the description of him (page 55). Answer the following questions.

a) What is Hans Holbein attempting to communicate about Sir Thomas More in the portrait? (*8 marks*)
b) What is Edward Hall attempting to communicate about Sir Thomas More in the description? (*4 marks*)
c) What, in the portrait and the description, suggests that the artist and the author had had first-hand experience of Sir Thomas More? (*3 marks*)

6. Allegory of the Reformation

Carefully study the woodcut Allegory of the Reformation from John Foxe's Book of Martyrs which is reproduced on page 45. Answer the following questions.

a) Why is the illustration referred to as an allegory? (*2 marks*)
b) Comment on the objects Henry VIII is shown holding in his hands. (*4 marks*)
c) Explain the messages that the artist was attempting to convey. (*9 marks*)

4 The Dissolution of the Monasteries

POINTS TO CONSIDER

As you read this chapter for the first time you need to concentrate on three aspects of this topic – often referred to as the '3Cs'. These are:
- causes (why the dissolution of the monasteries happened)
- course (what happened, organised into sections called 'stages') and
- consequences (the results of the dissolution of the monasteries).

KEY DATES

1535	*Valor Ecclesiasticus*; visitations to the monasteries
1536	Closure of the smaller monasteries; Pilgrimage of Grace
1538–40	Closure of the larger monasteries

1 Background

> **KEY ISSUES** What were monasteries in early sixteenth-century England? What was the popular attitude towards them?

When Henry VIII came to the throne in 1509 there were more than 850 religious houses in England and Wales. They are nowadays almost always referred to as monasteries, although the word was not common at the time. Many contemporary names were in use, often employed loosely and interchangeably, so that no hard and fast rules on terminology can be established. However, there was a tendency for the larger, mainly rural institutions to be called abbeys, for many of the medium-sized houses to be labelled priories or nunneries, and for the words friary and cell to be used to describe the smaller units.

The houses fell into one of two broad categories. There were those that were 'closed', in which the occupants – in theory at least – spent nearly all their time within the confines of the buildings and their adjacent fields and gardens, and devoted most of their energies to attending private religious services within their own chapel. The 'open' houses were the friaries, whose occupants were meant to work in the community at large, bringing spiritual comfort to the needy, be they the poor, the sick or merely those who were denied the services of an effective parish priest. The two categories were also distinguished by other differences. Whereas the friaries were confined to the towns or their environs, were almost always small, and were universally poor (it was against the rule of each of the four orders of friar to own property other than for their own immediate use), the 'closed' houses – now thought of as the typical monasteries – were more often situated in the countryside than in the towns, were frequently large (in their buildings if not in their number of occupants), and were generally rich.

In fact, the wealth of the 'typical' monasteries as a group was enormous. They possessed most of the Church's riches, normally estimated as including about one third of the country's landed property. For example, the 30 or so richest monasteries each received an income approximating to that of one of the country's most powerful nobles. This money was derived mainly from 'temporal' sources, but one 'spiritual' source was significant. The 'temporal' element was overwhelmingly made up of rents from the agricultural land that they owned, while the 'spiritual' mainly took the form of profits from the parish priesthoods (benefices) that they held. These arose because very often the monastery would employ a vicar or curate to do the parish work, while retaining the lion's share of the value of the benefice for its own use. A monastery had often acquired this wealth over several centuries, normally through dozens (in some cases even hundreds) of bequests made in the wills of property owners, large and small, in the hope that their generosity would lessen the time their souls would spend in purgatory.

Most monasteries had been in existence for many generations and were accepted as an integral part of the community by almost the entire population which, mostly disliking change and having grown up with the religious houses, unquestioningly assumed that they were a normal part of life. Although a significant minority of the population lived and died without ever having seen a monastery, most people lived close enough to one, or to one of its outlying estates, to be aware of its activities. And although there were probably no more than a few hundred itinerant preaching friars active at any one time, it is unlikely that many adults would have escaped contact with them at some point during their lives. What evidence there is suggests that in the first half of Henry VIII's reign the popular expectation was that monasteries would always continue to exist.

2 Wolsey's Dissolutions

> **KEY ISSUE** Was Wolsey's dissolution of monasteries at all remarkable?

However, during the 1520s Cardinal Wolsey was responsible for dissolving 29 small religious houses and for taking over their property with the stated intention of using it to pay for the foundation of a grammar school in his home town of Ipswich and a new college at his old university of Oxford. But there was nothing very remarkable or ominous in this. This was despite the fact that the scale of his activities was much greater than had been that of the bishops who had occasionally taken action to suppress individual religious houses during the past generation. All of the houses dissolved by Wolsey were 'decayed', in that they had ceased to be viable in the terms envisaged by their founders because of a decline in the number of monks or nuns they contained. Their endowments were to be used for alternative charitable purposes and the dissolutions were carried out totally legally and with explicit papal permission. The fact that the paperwork was not properly tied up by the time of Wolsey's fall in 1529, so that the property was transferred to the king along with all the other possessions of the Cardinal, was little known and certainly caused no public consternation. Nor, at that stage, could any significance be read into the fact that most of the detailed work on the dissolutions had been carried out by Wolsey's chief legal adviser, Thomas Cromwell.

3 The Visitation and the *Valor Ecclesiasticus* of 1535

> **KEY ISSUES** How were the Visitations carried out and the *Valor Ecclesiasticus* compiled? What was their importance?

Two overlapping processes, which were historically significant in their own right as well as yielding historians a mass of detailed information about the state of the monasteries at the time, took place in 1535. Cromwell was the king's vicegerent responsible for the day-to-day control of the Church. He planned for most religious houses to be visited by his representatives. Such visitations had long been accepted as a normal, if infrequent, way of ensuring that monasteries were conducting their affairs properly. Traditionally such visitations had been conducted under the authority of the bishop in whose diocese the house lay. In the case of the many houses that had been exempted from such control by a papal dispensation, the visitations had been carried out under the authority of the head of the Order to which the house belonged.

Although Cromwell's programme of visitations was only partial in that it did not include a large number of the smaller monasteries, it was not completed by the end of May as originally intended, and was barely finished by the end of the year. This was because it was interrupted by a second and even more ambitious undertaking, the *Valor Ecclesiasticus*. This was nothing less than an attempt to make a record of all the property owned by the Church in England and Wales, including the monasteries – a colossal undertaking given the lack of civil servants and the primitive state of much estate management at the time. The work was carried out by unpaid groups of commissioners, mainly local gentry, who, as far as the monasteries were concerned, visited all the religious houses in their county and, by asking questions and examining account books, built up a picture of the property owned by the monks, nuns or friars. Historians have been lavish in their praise of the completeness and accuracy of the Commissioners' work and the *Valor Ecclesiasticus* has been compared to the Domesday Book as an administrative achievement. Certainly, it has proved to be a bedrock for those researching either the dissolution of the monasteries or the subsequent history of the lands that were taken over by the Crown in the process.

However, it was the series of visitations that took place in 1535 that was of the greater significance at the time. Much of the work was carried out by two of Cromwell's trusted 'servants' (a word that would be better translated as 'employees' nowadays), Thomas Legh and Richard Layton. They shared many of the attributes of their master. They were very able (so that the wool could rarely be pulled over their eyes), were prodigious workers (as the speed at which they travelled around the country showed), were highly ambitious (realising that the only way to succeed was to give their superiors exactly what they wanted), and were completely unscrupulous when they needed to be (although they could be humane, and even generous, where their vital interests were not affected). From the letters they regularly sent to Cromwell describing their activities it is possible both to piece together their itinerary and to assess the way in which they worked. Before they left London they were provided with lists of questions to ask at each house and sets of instructions (injunctions) to issue the monks and nuns they 'visited' – both as appropriate. Although there is no direct evidence for this, it seems that they were also told to make as full a record as possible of all the shortcomings in the lives of the members of the religious houses. Certainly, the detailed *comperta* (lists of transgressions admitted by monks and nuns) that they compiled suggest that this was so. The short amount of time (often only hours) spent at many houses, the huge quantities of information collected and the many complaints about their bullying tactics, suggests that they were anything but gentle in their work. In the process they acquired a widespread reputation as typifying all that was bad in the government's new ways of conducting much of its business. They were even included in a list of the king's 'evil counsellors' thought to be deserving of special punishment, drawn up during the Pilgrimage of Grace in 1536.

4 The Dissolution of the Smaller Monasteries (1536)

> **KEY ISSUE** What is meant by 'the dissolution of the smaller monasteries'?

Ever since the visitation of 1535 and the commissions to compile the *Valor Ecclesiasticus* had begun, rumours had been rife that the government's intention was to disband the monasteries and to seize their wealth. These fears were born out in part by an act which was passed by parliament in March 1536. The act stipulated that all religious houses with an annual income of less than £200 (as assessed in the *Valor Ecclesiasticus*) should be dissolved and that their property should pass to the Crown. It provided for the heads of the houses to be granted a pension and for other members to be offered the option of transferring to a larger house or ceasing to be 'religious' by going out into the world without being bound by the vows of poverty and obedience that they had taken, although they were expected to continue to honour their vow of chastity and therefore would be unable to marry.

Just over 300 houses fell within the category specified by the act, but by no means all of them were immediately dissolved. The act had given the king power to grant exemptions to individual 'smaller' houses as he saw fit. Evidence has been found that he did so in 67 cases, and it is estimated that there were probably a further ten or more monasteries that escaped closure but whose records have been lost. What is known for certain is that those monasteries whose application for exemption was successful were forced to pay heavily – often in excess of a year's income – for the privilege. The official position was that the houses granted exemption were those worthy of continuation because of the high quality of their performance, but it seems in reality that the escapees were a mixture of those with friends in high places and those with a high percentage of members who wished to remain as monks or nuns. Apparently, the prospect of finding new 'homes' for hundreds of displaced religious was somewhat daunting to Cromwell and his leading assistants.

As soon as the legislation had received the royal assent commissions, whose task it was to implement the closure of the monasteries affected, were appointed to each county. The urgency was necessary to ensure that as little as possible of the monasteries' movable wealth disappeared before it could be seized for the Crown. In most districts the groups of commissioners acted speedily and efficiently. The monasteries to be dissolved were visited, any inmates who remained were expelled, valuable metal – especially gold, silver, lead from roofs and bronze from bells – was carted off, normally to the Tower of London, any saleable items (even down to hinges from doors) were auctioned locally, and any property that had not pre-viously been let out was offered to rent to a selection of the many people who rapidly came forward with requests for such favours. A large number of the monastic buildings were in such a poor state of repair that by the time locals had helped themselves to whatever the commissioners had not put up for sale, in many cases there was soon little to show that a monastery had previously existed on the site.

However, the 'vultures' did not descend equally speedily in all areas. Particularly in the counties of the north, widespread disap-proval of what was happening was more in evidence than individual greed. As a result, commissioners generally acted less energetically and were often willingly prevented from taking action by groups of local people who made it clear that they would offer physical violence to anybody who tried to implement the act. The groups of commis-sioners who ignored such warnings are thought to have been partly responsible for stirring up the Lincolnshire Rising and the Pilgrimage of Grace in October 1536. Certainly, once the rebellions were under way no further action could be taken to dissolve monasteries in the areas affected, and some of the houses which had already been closed were even re-opened (see Henry VIII and the Government of England in this series).

5 The Destruction of the Remaining Monasteries (1538–40)

> **KEY ISSUE** What methods were used to dissolve the larger monasteries?

Although most monasteries were careful to remain aloof from the Pilgrimage of Grace, a number were pressured into providing active support. These houses, large and small, were high on Henry VIII's vengeance list once order was restored. The technique used to punish them was thought at the time to be of dubious legality. The head of each house involved was declared a traitor in an act of attain-der passed by parliament (there was no trial) and was sentenced to be publicly executed, normally at his own monastery. The posses-sions of the house were treated as if they had belonged to the abbot personally, and were transferred to the king as was the case with all traitors. Any remaining monks not being punished for taking part in the rebellion, were forced to leave their homes and commissioners disposed of the house's assets in the way that had been normal in 1536.

Of course, this action left hundreds of surviving houses, mainly to the south and west of the river Trent. These included most of the rich-est and most famous monasteries in the land. However, by early 1540 none remained in existence. The process by which this massive change took place was piecemeal – there was no equivalent for the larger monasteries of the act of 1536. Once, in 1538, the dust from the Pilgrimage of Grace had fully settled, Cromwell sent out pairs of his most trusted servants with commissions to receive the property of the remaining religious houses as free gifts to the king. Each commission was for a specified part of the country, except that for the friaries which applied nationally. In their early 'sweeps' the commissioners were instructed to spend little time on those heads of houses and their communities who seemed prepared to resist strongly. They were merely to report such situations, having created as much fear and discord as possible, and to devote their energies to the vast majority of abbots and abbesses who were prepared to please the king. Many of the heads of houses who initially resisted the 'invitation' of the commissioners were willing to resign their positions when instructed to do so in their monarch's name. They were then speedily replaced by men and women who were known to be more amenable, with the obvious end result.

Part way through the sequence of sweeps there occurred an event of only technical significance. In 1539 an act of parliament was passed stipulating that any voluntary surrenderings of monastic property which had so far taken place, or which were to take place in the future, were completely legal and that no challenges to the validity of the king's title to the possessions – or of those to whom he subsequently transferred them – were to be allowed by the courts. This virtual afterthought had been enacted because some of Henry's legal advisers were fearful that without it the way would be open to potentially embarrassing legal disputes in the future. But, of course, the passage of the act neither speeded up nor slowed down the pace at which the dissolutions took place.

Despite the overwhelming success of the commissioners, there was a handful of individual heads of houses who, with the support of their communities, were not prepared to be cajoled or frightened into compliance. They were the stuff of which martyrs are made, and Henry did not disappoint their expectations. They were tried on spurious charges of treachery – normally for crimes such as secreting items of value so that they would not eventually fall into the king's hands – and were sentenced to death, with the possessions of their houses being forfeited to the Crown. The most famous to suffer in this way were the Abbots of Colchester, Reading and Glastonbury. The latter was the head of one of the richest monasteries in the country. His execution at his abbey, along with the subsequent destruction of one of the finest buildings in England, was for generations to be one of the best remembered 'crimes' of Henry VIII. The flavour of how the abbot's downfall was brought about can be gained from extracts from a letter written to Cromwell by the commissioners who visited Glastonbury in 1539:

1 ... and then proceeded to search his [the abbot's] study for letters and
books; and found in his study secretly laid, as well a written book or
argument against the divorce of the King's Majesty and the lady dowager [Catherine of Aragon], which we take to be a great matter, as also
5 divers pardons, copies of bulls, and the counterfeit life of Thomas
Becket in print: but we could not find any letter that was material. And
so we proceeded again to his examination concerning the articles we
received from your Lordship, in the answers whereof, as we take it,
shall appear his cankered and traitorous heart against the King's Majesty
10 and his succession ... we have found a fair chalice of gold, and divers
other parcels of plate, which the abbot had hid secretly from all such
commissioners as have been there in times past; and as yet he knoweth
not that we have found the same.

The dissolution of over 800 monasteries in less than five years is a
remarkably well-documented episode, thanks mainly to the survival of
the letters received by Cromwell from the men responsible for carrying out the work. As a result, historians have long been in very general agreement about what happened and when. In recent decades
the researches of local historians have usefully filled out many of the
details, but they have done little to amend the overall picture.
However, the same degree of unanimity has never existed in providing answers to the 'why?' and 'with what effects?' questions. These
have for long been part of the battleground of the 'What sort of king
was Henry VIII?', 'What was the role of Thomas Cromwell?' and 'Why
was there a Reformation in England?' controversies.

6 Why were the Monasteries Dissolved?

> **KEY ISSUES** What were the Catholic and Protestant
> interpretations which were popular until about 1950? What is
> now the generally accepted interpretation?

a) The Early Sectarian Controversy

For about 300 years after the death of Henry VIII this was a hotly disputed question between writers with Catholic or Protestant sympa-
thies. The Catholics argued that the dissolution had nothing to do
with religion. Their contention was that a greedy and wicked king was
persuaded by his unscrupulous minister that a major piece of
legalised theft would make him wealthy almost beyond his wildest
dreams. They made much of a remark in a report of the Emperor's
ambassador, Eustace Chapuy, that Cromwell had risen to favour by
promising Henry that he would make him the richest king in
Christendom. They also attempted to prove that the monasteries were

generally functioning well and were respected by the population as a whole at the time of their destruction. They made much of the active support for the monasteries that was forthcoming in the north, especially during the Pilgrimage of Grace, and highlighted the bravery of those who chose to die rather than to comply with the sacrilegious orders of their king.

The Protestants argued that by the 1530s the monasteries were generally corrupt places where sinners and charlatans lived in degenerate luxury, paid for by the charitable bequests of earlier generations. In addition, they contended that the very raison d'être of the monastic way of life was based on one of the major lies that the Papacy had long ago promulgated in order to strengthen its own position. This was that merit in the eyes of God (and therefore salvation) was to be gained by good works rather than by faith, and that the highest form of good works was the living of a life devoted to worship, and especially the celebration of the Mass. To this ancient falsehood, they argued, had been added the fictional doctrine of purgatory, by which it was taught that the souls of the dead suffered agonies for a finite number of years before being admitted to heaven, and that the time spent in purgatory could be shortened by giving money to monks and nuns so that they would pray on your behalf. Therefore, their argument was that the monasteries deserved to be dissolved both because the money to support them had been acquired under false pretences and because they no longer carried out the functions that their founders had intended.

Protestant writers were also particularly keen to establish that the dissolution of the monasteries was an integral part of the Reformation in England. This they saw as a coherent process by which a debased form of Christianity emanating from Rome was replaced by a cleansed and revitalised version – the Church of England – thanks to the actions of Henry VIII, two of his children, and their ever more numerous Protestant supporters. In this the destruction of monastic ways of life was seen as important in that it rid the country of the major centres of support for the perverted belief that salvation could be gained by good works alone and, in particular, through a life devoted to worship and the avoidance of the world's temptations by shutting oneself away from them. Thus monasticism was viewed as an open challenge to the central Protestant belief that salvation was freely available to all those who were prepared to accept it by believing in God and his only son Jesus Christ. In these circumstances it was readily assumed that the monasteries must have been dissolved for 'religious' reasons, as part of the cleansing operation of the Reformation.

b) The Later Sectarian Controversy

As might be imagined, up to the middle of the nineteenth century this controversy generated much more heat than light, with most of those who took part in it being much more interested in defending a pre-determined position than in establishing any objective truth. The change during the next hundred years was that, although most writers still maintained an identifiably Catholic or Protestant position, a genuine attempt was made to substantiate their claims with facts. But because so many 'facts' existed that could be used to support either position, the dispute based on religious affiliation continued for much longer than might otherwise have been expected. Catholic writers were able to point to the extensive evidence of thriving spirituality within the English monastic system at the time of the dissolution. In particular they could catalogue the heroic struggle of so many members of the London Charterhouse (see page 52) and the complimentary reports about the virtue of much of what they found that were written by several of the groups of commissioners whose task it was to implement the closure of the smaller houses in 1536. They were also able to present further evidence that both Henry VIII and Thomas Cromwell were primarily motivated by greed in their decision to destroy the monasteries. In particular, they took pleasure in drawing attention to the fact that Cromwell made a conscious effort to enrich himself at the monasteries' expense. Not only did he accept 'gifts' from many smaller monasteries in return for supporting their appeals to be exempt from the terms of the 1536 act, but he also persuaded at least 30 religious houses to grant him an annual payment. The advantage of these retainers was that he could continue to claim them for the rest of his life, even after the monasteries involved were dissolved. The earliest known of them is typical of the rest:

1 Know that we, the aforesaid Abbot, hath given, granted, and by this our present writing confirm to Thomas Cromwell esquire, for his good and gratuitous counsel and aid, and for his goodwill already shown to us and to be shown, an annual rent or annuity of 26 shillings and 8 pence ster-
5 ling ... the abovementioned Thomas Cromwell to have, hold and receive the aforesaid annual rent ... during his lifetime ... Given 4 June in the twenty-third year of the reign of Henry VIII, by the grace of God of England and France King, Defender of the Faith, and Lord of Ireland.

However, Protestant authors were able to call upon much more extensive evidence to support their contention that the monasteries deserved to be closed. The *Valor Ecclesiasticus* and the comperta resulting from the visitations of 1535 provided a massive amount of ammunition. The *Valor Ecclesiasticus*, which itemised expenditure as well as income, could be used to show a major misapplication of monastic funds. It was calculated that, on average, about one quarter of each monastery's income was paid directly to the head of the house. This person, normally with the title of abbot or abbess, was in most cases an absentee leader, living the life of a country gentleman in a comfortable house on one of the monastery's manors, while leaving the day-to-day exercise of his or her duties to a deputy (normally called the prior or prioress) who was resident in the monastery. It was a simple matter to contrast this profligacy with the 3 per cent of income that the same document showed as being spent on charitable works. Even more damning, and certainly more sensational, was the story of widespread immorality and sexual perversion that could be extracted from the comperta. There were contemporary reports that it was the reading out of such evidence by ministers during the debate in the Commons on the legislation to dissolve the smaller monasteries which provoked angry support for the government's policy. That hundreds of monks had admitted to taking part in homosexual practices, often with young boys, while many others told of their strings of mistresses – accounts mirrored by the confessions of nuns to bearing children, sometimes several times – seemed to suggest that the isolated anecdotes of sexual laxity or worse that had been in circulation for decades were part of a general picture of moral depravity among the religious.

Writers approaching the issue from a Protestant standpoint have also been eager to establish that the monasteries were unpopular at the time of their dissolution. They have been able to point to general trends such as the decline in the number of men and women wishing to become monks or nuns in the final decades of the monasteries' existence, the hostility shown by MPs to the religious houses and their shortcomings, and the alacrity with which people from all walks of life attempted to acquire the monasteries' possessions once it seemed likely that they would become available. In addition, it has been possible to argue convincingly that by the 1530s the élite of leading English intellectuals, who might have been expected to feature among the monasteries' principal defenders, had reached the conclusion that the monastic way of life had little to commend it. Erasmus's scathing attacks on the lives lived by the religious had done much to bring about this negative perception of monasticism among the country's intellectual leaders, which seemingly had already percolated down to many of the less-educated members of the ruling élite. There have also been clear-cut cases of specific unpopularity to be discovered. Typical of these is a situation described in a petition found among Thomas Cromwell's papers. Among the complaints contained in it are the following:

1   the Prior of Plympton [in Devon] ... doth make and has made of the parish of Wembury to the sum of £50 sterling and the said parish hath not with them no priest uprising neither downlying [resident], not within the space of four miles of the said parish, but that if they have

5   need of a priest they must go to Plympton after him, the which is eight miles going and coming to the said parish ... And bear witness at all times that there hath been many one dead and hath died without shrift and housel [the eucharist] or any other sacrament ministered unto them.

10   And the said parish hath been without a priest many Sundays and

holy days in the year in times past so that they have had neither mass, matins nor evensong said to them.

Also, we of the said parish, considering how many times we have lacked a priest, and could never have one to our need, have hired a
15 priest at our own proper costs and charges, and the Prior not therewith satisfied nor content did send his steward and his bailiff to the said parish of Wembury and they commanded his tenants that if any of them did give anything to the priest's wages that they should forfeit their holdings. The which priest hath served with us for the space of ten
20 years.

c) Modern Interpretations

Most historians writing about the issue since the Second World War have had neither a Catholic nor a Protestant axe to grind and, although there have been clear differences of emphasis between them, a surprising degree of consensus has emerged.

The most significant point of agreement has been that the monasteries were dissolved almost entirely because Henry VIII wished to lay his hands on their wealth. Other contributory factors have been identified (and often disagreed about), but the vital factor – in that without it the dissolution would not have taken place – has generally, and most probably finally, been agreed to be the king's desire to acquire the monasteries' riches. In this the 'top-down' school, led by Elton and Scarisbrick, has been as one with the 'bottom-up' revisionists, including Dickens who was their original inspiration.

The 'top-down' historians reached this conclusion after finding that Henry was solidly behind each of the moves forward in the story of the dissolution, while at the same time accepting none of the doctrinaire reasons subsequently advanced by Protestants to justify his actions. Even more persuasive evidence that Henry's motives were not in the least 'religious' has been provided by the fact that he seems to have believed quite strongly in the traditional values of monasticism. Not only did he insist, against the wishes of his advisers, that the monks and nuns who chose to abandon their vocation when their houses were dissolved must be forced to maintain their vows of chastity, but he even went to the lengths of re-founding two monasteries after the initial batch of dissolutions with the specific purpose of ensuring that frequent prayers were said for him, his wife and the souls of his ancestors. At the same time, any possibility of the contention being successfully advanced that he supported the dissolution programme for general political reasons has been destroyed. It is clear that by mid-1535 any threat to the acceptance of either the royal supremacy or the new order of succession that the monasteries might have posed had effectively been eliminated. And Henry was clearly not impressed by the argument that, despite the monks and nuns having taken the oaths required of them, the monasteries would constitute a latent source of opposition as long as they were allowed to continue in existence.

The 'bottom-up' writers have reached the same position by establishing that there was very little popular opposition to the continued existence of the religious houses, and that their shortcomings were such that a modest reform programme could have eliminated most of them. In this, by chance, they have found themselves in agreement with some of the arguments previously advanced by Catholic historians. They have been able to prove beyond reasonable doubt that the public attitude towards the religious houses was just on the supportive side of neutral – that in any opinion poll (had such things existed at the time) the 'do not really mind one way or the other' would have been in a majority and that those strongly supportive or violently opposed to the continuation of the monasteries would have formed small minorities, with the latter probably being the smallest of all. This lack of strength of feeling against the monasteries is perhaps best exemplified by contrasting what happened in England and Wales with events in Germany. In Henry VIII's realm there were no examples of violence being offered to existing religious houses and their inmates, while in Germany the sacking of monasteries by hostile mobs intent on ending what they regarded as anti-Christian practices commonly accompanied the spread of the Reformation into new districts. It even seems that in England and Wales those who complained about specific abuses which adversely affected them were content merely to grumble and were generally in favour of the monastic system as a whole. They, in common with most of the population, appear to have accepted as a fact of life the way in which the abbots and abbesses took such a high percentage of their houses' income. There is no indication of widespread indignation and it is likely that if the man in the street had been asked for his opinion about the situation he would have said 'Lucky old them'.

The 'bottom-up' historians have also shown that the state of the monasteries in the 1530s was not nearly as bad as Protestant writers have generally maintained. Their conclusion has been that, although less than 10 per cent of houses were centres of spiritual fervour, the vast majority were adequately following the way of life prescribed by the Order to which they belonged. In particular, they have established that the comperta resulting from the visitations of 1535 must be treated with extreme caution. It is clear that the visitors carried out their orders to 'dig up as much dirt as possible' with efficiency and enthusiasm, but with no regard for fairness or presenting a balanced picture. Although it is not suggested that they went as far as fabricating evidence, there is no doubt that they were prepared to mislead quite outrageously. This can be shown both from internal evidence in their reports and from external evidence that has been unearthed relating to a few of the confessions included in the comperta. It was the reporting of a total of 181 cases of 'sodomy' that gave rise to claims of widespread homosexual practices in monasteries. But a careful reading of the reports shows that the visitors' definition of sodomy was most unusual, in that all but 12 of the cases are described as being instances of 'solitary vice', presumably masturbation. Thus, in fact, there was one confession of homosexuality for roughly every 30 monasteries visited. There were 38 confessions by nuns that they had had children. But it is now known that one of the pregnancies took place at the beginning of the century, and probably before the nun in question took her vow of chastity. This opens the possibility that many of the other confessions related to similarly ancient falls from grace. It is therefore clear that the religious houses were in no sense the dens of vice that they have sometimes been painted as being.

Thus the currently agreed explanation of the causes of the dissolution of the monasteries is well-rounded and convincing in its essentials. It is clear that there was no popular demand for the destruction of the religious houses, that they were not in a terminal state of collapse through decadence and moral laxity, and that they posed no political or religious threat to the king or his policies. However, they did possess enormous wealth, and it was the desire to gain control of this that motivated Henry to allow or to insist that Cromwell and his assistants destroyed the monasteries and transferred their possessions to the Crown.

7 How far was the Dissolution of the Monasteries pre-planned?

> **KEY ISSUES** What arguments can be put forward to support the claims that Henry and Cromwell i) planned the dissolution of the monasteries from the outset, and, ii) merely took advantage of opportunities as they arose? 'On balance of probability' where does the truth lie?

For nearly 400 years after the event it was the received wisdom among writers on the subject who were hostile to Henry VIII that Cromwell had risen to power by promising the king to acquire the wealth of the monasteries for him, and that he spent the next seven or eight years putting his plan into operation. Thus, the belief was that the end result was in mind from the outset. It was argued that the proposal's successful outcome was assured once the king had given it his blessing. Such a simplistic view can no longer be supported.

The central, three-stage thread of the interpretation – that Cromwell offered, that Henry VIII accepted and that Cromwell delivered – is very much open to question. In particular, few people would now support the suggestion that Cromwell ever made an explicit offer to Henry VIII about the monasteries. The evidence that he did so is highly unreliable, being based on hostile gossip some time after the event, and, in any case, the story portrays Cromwell in a role that was foreign to him. He did not do deals with Henry – the relationship was much too unequal for that – and any planting of ideas that he did was by subtle insinuation, probably in casual conversation, over a period of time, for it was essential that Henry believed any new idea to be his own. Nor is it likely that Cromwell would have needed to introduce the possibility of dissolution to Henry, who was well-informed as well as greedy, and would probably have heard about the seizures of monastic land in Lutheran Germany, Zwinglian Switzerland, Denmark and Sweden before he ever met Cromwell. It is likely that his imagination would have been set racing by such news.

Of course, the truth of what happened will never be known – the evidence does not exist – but a well-informed guess would be that the king and his minister discovered in conversation together that they shared a common perception that there was money to be made from a well-timed dissolution of some monasteries. It is likely that this happened later rather than sooner, probably about the middle of 1535. Certainly, there seems to have been no intention to implement a programme of dissolutions on the part of either man at the beginning of the year when Cromwell initiated the visitation of the monasteries and Henry ordered the collection of the information that was to become the *Valor Ecclesiasticus*. Cromwell probably had a wide range of motives for deciding to exercise his rights of visitation as vicegerent. Among these might have been a desire to have his powers understood throughout the country (often a slow process in the days before the mass media), a genuine wish to reform the monasteries in an evangelical direction (the fact that he ordered all monks and nuns regularly to listen both to the Bible read in English and to sermons based on it suggests this), and a plan to enrich himself at the monasteries' expense by ordering them to obey impossibly restrictive regulations and then granting them exemptions in return for cash 'gifts'. This much can be surmised from the injunctions that his representatives were instructed to issue to each house. Among these were:

> 4 Also that no monk or brother of this monastery by any means go forth of the precincts of the same.
>
> 5 Also that women, of what state or degree soever they be, be utterly excluded from entering into the limits or circuit of this monastery or place unless they first obtain licence of the King's highness or his visitor.
>
> 6 Also that there be no entering into this monastery but one and that by the great fore-gate of the same.
>
> 15 Also that the Abbot or President [resident head of the house] keep and find in some university one or two of his brethren, according to the ability and possessions of this house, which brethren after they be

learned in good and holy letters when they return home may instruct and teach their brethren and diligently preach the word of God.

23 Also that they shall not show any relics or feigned miracles for
15 increase of lucre but that they exhort pilgrims and strangers to give that to the poor that they thought to offer to their images or relics.

Certainly, it is most probable that the instruction to the visitors to gather as much evidence as possible of the monasteries' shortcomings was issued later in the year, suggesting that it was only then that the king had decided that a partial dissolution was soon to take place. And, although the *Valor Ecclesiasticus* was to be a vital tool in implementing the dissolution of the smaller monasteries, it was certainly not designed with this in mind. Its purpose was to provide the information necessary to calculate how much each institution would have to pay as the 10 per cent of clerical income that parliament had already granted Henry (see page 40). Had seizure of property been in mind questions would have been asked about the liquid assets (in cash and kind) held by each monastery.

The fact that Cromwell had not had time to draw together all the evidence against the smaller monasteries by the time parliament came to debate the legislation dissolving them suggests that the minister was not working according to a carefully laid plan. It is much more likely that he was having to react to a sequence of his master's hastily made decisions – even though they were decisions of which he heartily approved and which he had probably done much to encourage.

A strong case can be made to support the contention that the dissolution of the smaller monasteries in 1536 was envisaged by Henry and Cromwell as a one-off 'smash and grab' operation. In it as much wealth as possible would be secured for the Crown from those religious houses which could be argued to be too small to be truly viable, as proved by the lack of discipline uncovered by the previous year's visitations. They probably judged that this move would be acceptable to the propertied classes, whose support they needed to retain, because it was merely a small extension of the long-held clerical belief that a religious house of less than a head and 12 members was too small to be effective. It was true that the head-count approach was being replaced by a criterion based on income (houses with an income of less than £200 pa were to be dissolved), but it could be maintained (not very honestly) that the result would be essentially the same.

Certainly, the wording of the 1536 act would lead one to think that a total dissolution of the monasteries was not envisaged, even as a long-term aim. The entire document revolved around the claim that by weeding out the smaller religious houses, in which the monastic life was not and could not be effectively pursued, and by transferring dedicated monks and nuns to the larger houses which were in a good state of spiritual health, any necessary reform of the system would be achieved:

1 ... so that without such small houses be utterly suppressed and the religious persons therein committed to great and honourable monasteries
  of religion in this realm, where they may be compelled to live
  religiously, for reformation of their lives, there can else be no reforma-
5 tion in this behalf:
  ... considering also that divers and great solemn monasteries of this
  realm wherein (thanks be to God) religion is right well kept and
  observed, be destitute of such full numbers of religious persons as they
  ought and may keep ...

However, this seemingly clear evidence is not to be trusted. Much of
the legislation instigated by the government during the 1530s was
couched in terms that were mere propaganda, in that the arguments
used were those that it was thought would be acceptable. In fact they
were often the complete opposite of the government's motivation or
of what was intended for the future. This means that the wording of
the 1536 act is essentially worthless as evidence of either Henry and
Cromwell's motives for dissolving the smaller monasteries or their
plans regarding the larger ones.

Nor should the fact that no further action was taken until 1538 be
thought to have any bearing on the question of whether or not there
was any long-term plan to dissolve all the monasteries. The inaction is
totally explicable in terms of Henry's decision to slow down the pace
of change and Cromwell's wish to lie as low as possible following the
widespread discontent with government policies that had been
revealed by the Pilgrimage of Grace in late 1536. But this is not to
argue that there was a plan. In fact, both the sequence of events that
followed the dissolution of the smaller monasteries and what is known
of Henry and Cromwell's methods of working lead to the same conclusion: that, on balance of probability (the evidence will support no
stronger claim than this), the government was merely taking advantage of possibilities as they somewhat unexpectedly arose.

The key to the situation appears to have been the news received by
Cromwell that many of the larger monasteries were expecting to be
dissolved in the near future and were dispersing their assets among
friends and well-wishers so that they would not fall into the king's
hands. This seems to have caused Cromwell to amend his judgement
that the richer religious houses would be too powerful to destroy without risking widespread political unrest. The 'sweep' of late 1538 and
early 1539 was probably a move to test the resolve of the remaining
monasteries. When it was found that most were willing to surrender
without a struggle, it was an obvious encouragement to press on with
the process. It would have been typical of Henry, now made aware
that huge riches were his for the taking, to instruct his minister to
complete the dissolution, even if it meant taking violent action against
the resisters. He would have found no difficulty in justifying to himself the virtually overnight change from wishing to found new monasteries to pray on his behalf to insisting on the destruction of all

religious houses, whatever their spiritual merits. Equally it would have been very typical of Cromwell, the highly skilled, pragmatic politician, both to have seized on a half-opportunity and to have converted it into a huge success, and to have learned from the events of 1536 that it was safer to pick off his intended victims one by one rather than by launching a full-frontal attack.

Of course, it could never be proved that Henry and Cromwell had not planned the destruction of all the monasteries from the outset, but it seems unlikely that they did. Henry's actions, in particular, fit the pattern of the bold adventurer who intended to steal half the apples and then found that the rest virtually fell into his lap. It is more possible that Cromwell dreamt of a complete dissolution from the early 1530s onwards, (he had that sort of mind), but he certainly possessed no blueprint for turning such an aspiration into reality. His achievement – if it can be regarded as such – was in taking initiatives whenever the slightest opportunity arose, and following them through with outstanding administrative skill. No one else of his generation could have done it so well.

8 Why was there so little Resistance to the Dissolution?

> **KEY ISSUES** What advantages did Henry VIII possess? What use did he make of his advantages?

When the Protestant interpretation of rotten and unpopular monasteries collapsing with the slightest of nudges from Henry VIII held sway, there was no need to explain the fact that the religious houses disappeared without there being widespread civil unrest. But since the accepted orthodoxy is now that the dissolution was an act of state carried out against reasonably healthy institutions which enjoyed general support, the issue has become much more relevant. It has become necessary to provide an explanation for the ease with which Henry and Cromwell got their way.

In fact, it has not proved difficult to identify the reasons once the nature of English society at the time has been properly appreciated.

By the 1530s the general respect ('awe' or even 'fear' would be equally appropriate words) for the power of the monarch, which had been growing since the accession of Henry VII 45 years earlier, had reached such proportions that a determined English king could do virtually whatever he wanted. This deference was even apparent in rebels, such as the leaders of the Pilgrimage of Grace in 1536, and was possibly the major cause of their undoing (see Henry VIII and the Government of England in this series for a discussion of this issue). This gave Henry a tremendous advantage in his dealings with all of his subjects, the heads of religious houses included. When there is added to this the fact that the king was known to be willing to use the power of the law – in effect, judicial murder – against all who opposed his will, it took very brave and committed people to fail to comply with their sovereign's wishes. And, of course, Henry had the law on his side in another way during his dealings with the monasteries. Parliament had recognised his position as Supreme Head of the Church in his territories and thus his authority over the religious houses and their possessions. He was therefore within his rights in dealing with them as he saw fit, a position that the monks and nuns had sworn an oath to accept in 1535.

But it was not only the king's exalted position and the might of the law that potential opponents within the monastic system had to confront. After 1536 they also had to overcome the lure of a large element of self-interest. This was because Cromwell was careful to make it financially worth the while of heads of houses to surrender their monasteries into the Crown's hands. It was left to the commissioners negotiating the surrender to agree on the exact terms, but the principle to be followed was that the abbots and abbesses should not be significantly worse off after the dissolution than they had been before. This, of course, was expensive to implement in the early years but as all grants were only for life there was the prospect of the allowances being recovered within a relatively short time. When the larger monasteries were being dissolved steps were also taken to discourage rank-and-file resistance. If the income of the house could finance it – and in all cases except the friaries it could – the ordinary monks and nuns were to be awarded a pension for life, which in practice was roughly equivalent to the wages of a manual worker. An added advantage of this arrangement was that heads of houses were freed from any feeling that they were sentencing the members of their communities to extreme hardship if they chose to sign the surrender papers when they were invited to do so.

It used to be commonplace to assert that the lay supporters of the monasteries, especially within the court circle, were bought off by the hint that they would be allowed to share in the spoils from the dissolution. While it is clear that such expectations were raised, it is very unlikely that they played a significant part in defusing potential political opposition. Henry ensured that few laymen would seriously contemplate even speaking out about the dissolution of the monasteries by making it clear that the penalty for doing so was likely to be death. In addition, once the opportunity of stopping the dissolutions had been missed in parliament in 1536, Cromwell made certain that by his policy of piecemeal surrenders he denied his opponents an obvious time at which to make a stand. In these circumstances, the hope of financial gain for themselves was merely a sweetener to those who wished the monasteries to remain.

9 What were the Effects of the Dissolution?

> **KEY ISSUES** What is the traditional view about the short-term effects of the dissolution? How has this view been modified in recent times? What suggestions have been made about the probable long-term effects of the dissolution? How convincing are these suggestions?

For centuries Catholic writers criticised the dissolution for its religious, humanitarian and cultural effects. The word 'vandalism' was much used – 'religious' vandalism because institutions with a proud spiritual tradition going back many centuries were eliminated at a time when they were far from moribund and when there were even signs of a significant upsurge of piety, and 'cultural' vandalism because many of the realm's most impressive pieces of medieval architecture were wilfully destroyed and most of its finest examples of medieval art, (the illustrated manuscripts in monastery libraries), were carelessly allowed to be lost because their contents were temporarily out of fashion. Much was also made of the hardships suffered by the occupants of the dissolved monasteries. It was claimed that their ordered way of life was suddenly ended when they were cast out into a turbulent and fast-changing world. It was also said that the many poor people who had depended on the charity disbursed by the religious houses suffered considerable hardship as a result of the dissolution.

Modern historians recognise a large element of special pleading in this argument. In particular, the cries of religious vandalism are seen to be largely subjective, being dependent on the writer's value system, and as such worthy of little consideration by professional researchers of history, in whom objectivity is expected to prevail. After all, committed Protestant writers have advanced an exactly opposite point of view. It is, of course, very difficult to make an objective assessment of the religious effect of the dissolution. What criteria does one apply, and what relevant evidence exists? These are issues that have not greatly interested recent historians of the English Reformation, who have generally satisfied themselves with the judgement that the dissolution of the monasteries was probably the part of the Reformation that had the least effect on either the quality or the quantity of religion in England and Wales. The claim of cultural vandalism has generally been treated more sympathetically, although probably with more subjectivity than objectivity. There is a strong streak of 'if it is old it must be worth retaining' sentimentality running throughout the Western world, and the sight of the majestic ruins of some of the larger rural abbeys, such as Fountains in Yorkshire and Tintern in Gwent, still elicits criticism of the action that resulted in such a loss of architectural heritage. Of course, it should be remembered that not all was lost. In particular, abbey churches survived to become cathedrals in the new dioceses such as Bristol, Gloucester, Chester and Westminster, while several others were purchased by their local communities to serve as parish churches. It may or may not be a relevant fact that few of the hundreds of monastic buildings that disappeared, leaving no trace above ground that they ever existed, are thought to have possessed any distinctive (let alone unique) architectural merit.

The claim that considerable humanitarian harm was done by the dissolution has excited considerable interest among modern historians and has been the subject of a large amount of painstaking research. Much of this has taken the form of tracking down what happened to named individuals who were turned out into the world by the dissolution. In their totality, the findings of the researchers have been surprisingly clear-cut, even allowing for their incompleteness and the possibility of a high margin of error. The conclusion reached has been that all but about 1500 of the 8000 monks and friars who were dispossessed by the dissolution managed to find alternative paid employment within the Church with which to supplement their pensions, thus allowing them to live comfortably if not luxuriously. It has been estimated that the majority of the 2000 nuns affected by the dissolution did less well, as they were neither allowed to marry nor were eligible for the priestly posts that were the refuge of many of their male counterparts. It is not known how many of them were able to return to their original families, but those who could not were probably forced to live at a very basic subsistence level, although there was no need for them to starve. No quantitative evidence is available about either the lay servants of the monasteries or the poor who had benefited from monastic charity on either a regular or a casual basis. However, it is thought likely that the majority of servants would have been able to find employment with the new lessees or owners of the monasteries' property, while the disappearance of monastic alms is considered to have added to an already serious problem rather than to have caused a new one. The plight of the poor was already dire on a national scale and it is likely that the ending of the monasteries' charitable activities was merely one of many reasons why the problem was becoming high on the government's list of major worries. Tudor Economy and Society in this series contains a fuller discussion of this and the following points.

Thus the recent tendency among historians has been to play down the traditional arguments of the Catholic writers about the effects of the dissolution. The same is true of some of the other traditionally asserted negative effects. It used to be claimed that the transfer of the monastic estates to a new breed of capitalist, 'make high profits at any cost' farmers resulted in thousands of their tenants being squeezed to pay higher rents which they could only do by accepting a significantly lower standard of living for themselves, and that by enclosing large amounts of land in order to make it more profitable to farm they were responsible for causing large-scale depopulation and homelessness. Modern local and regional studies aimed at examining these contentions have shown them to be largely unfounded. It has been discovered that not only were the rents charged by the new possessors of monastic estates generally similar to those imposed by the former owners, but also that nearly all the enclosure of monastic land took place before the dissolution rather than after it. Similarly, the old contention that the destruction of the monasteries led to the urban decay that was a feature of mid-Tudor England has been shown to be inaccurate. Although it is true that some towns did possess a large number of religious houses, – there were 23 in London alone – in every case that has been studied the disappearance of the expenditure generated by the monks, nuns and friars has been assessed as having a minimal impact on the prosperity of the community as a whole. If towns were experiencing problems it was not because the monasteries had ceased to exist. Thus it would seem that recent historians have gone a long way towards discrediting traditional beliefs about the short-term effects of the dissolution.

When considering the possible long-term consequences of the dissolution, historians have traditionally focused attention on the effect of the disappearance of the monasteries on the relative wealth of the Crown. This is because the seizures made between 1536 and 1540 had the potential of virtually doubling the king's normal income and of freeing him from any dependence on parliamentary grants, except in very exceptional circumstances. The political significance of this possibility was not lost on those writing after the seventeenth century, when the emergence of a parliamentary monarchy rather than the development of a European-style royal despotism was thought to have largely been the result of the Crown's relative poverty. The orthodoxy became that Henry VIII squandered an opportunity to ensure the Crown's long-term financial independence, where a wiser monarch (such as his father) would not have done. There are several flaws in this 'old' view. The most obvious of these is that the writers who have advanced it have been guilty of exercising that most dangerous of tools – hindsight. There is no doubt that Henry was deeply concerned about the future of the monarchy, and of his dynasty in particular. Otherwise his actions over potential rival claimants to his throne (see chapter 5 of Henry VIII and the Government of England for details) and the lengths he went to in an attempt to ensure that he left an adult male heir to succeed him would make no sense. But he had no reason to imagine that the future of the monarchy might depend on financial independence from parliament. After all, he regarded the institution as a useful and pliant adjunct to his power. His experience was that it always did what he wanted it to, as long as his demands were tactfully presented, and he had no reason to think that the situation would ever change. Certainly, he can not be blamed for failing to realise that the Commons would ever be a threat to the monarchy.

The other major flaw in the traditional 'squandering' argument is the contention that Henry gave away a significant proportion of the monastic wealth that should have come to him. Detailed research into what happened to the estates of the dissolved monasteries has proved that this was just not so. The picture that has emerged is of a miserly monarch, encouraged by Cromwell, who gave away virtually nothing. It is true that by the time of Henry's death about one half of the monastic lands had left royal possession permanently, but nearly all of it – even that acquired by his friends – had been sold at a full market price. It seems that the only favour the king was prepared to grant to those who 'had his ear' was to permit them or their friends to purchase the estates they wanted rather than allowing rival bidders to be successful. At one time it was thought that the existence of buyers who rapidly sold on the estates they purchased proved that the Crown disposed of the land too cheaply – otherwise there would have been no profit for the 'middle man' to make – but even this argument has been shown to be fallacious. It seems that the 'middle men' were merely acting as agents for the real purchasers and were earning no more than a modest fee from their activities.

The real argument that remains is whether Henry was wise in his spending of the half of the monastic wealth he disposed of, given that he and his ministers had already ensured that they maximised the value of the assets they sold. Here there is unlikely ever to be agreement. Most of the money realised from the sale of monastic land was spent on the wars against France and Scotland that were fought in the last years of Henry's reign. We now know that the wars achieved nothing of substance for Henry or his subjects and could have been avoided had the king wished to do so. In the light of these facts, most commentators will choose to accuse Henry of wasteful folly or worse. However, there is an alternative defensible point of view. This involves making a judgement as if from Henry's point of view at the time. Applying such criteria, would it have been justifiable for Henry not to spend the money as he did, when he believed that a monarch's first duty was to be victorious in battle and when he could see the possibility of adding one or even two kingdoms to the lands he already possessed? And, after all, when he died he did leave behind him about a half of the additional wealth he had acquired.

However, there is one area in which it is now generally agreed that the dissolution had very significant long-term consequences. This is in the social sphere. Because so much of the monastic land was sold by Henry VIII and during the reigns of Edward VI and Elizabeth I (virtually none remained in royal possession in 1603), the number of estates available to be bought was much greater than at any time for centuries. Although many of the manors were purchased by those who already owned considerable estates, many were bought by those who would otherwise have remained 'landless' and therefore inferior to the existing country gentlemen. Some of these were merchants

Summary Diagram
The Dissolution of the Monasteries

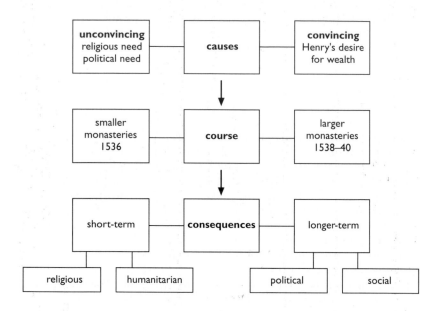

who had made their money from trade but more were the younger sons of landowning families who, because of the system of primogeniture by which the eldest son inherited all the land owned by his father, were otherwise doomed to drop out of the social élite into which they had been born. The effect of this was to increase the number of those enjoying the social rank of country gentleman by several thousand before the end of the century. Some would argue that it was this enlargement of the land-owning class which resulted in England becoming a parliamentary monarchy, freer from violent revolution than its European neighbours and with the tradition of slow and peaceful change that is such an important part of our heritage.

Thus it seems that the effects of the dissolution of the monasteries might have been very significant indeed in the long term, but not in the short term and not for the course of the Reformation in England. It has even been suggested that the Reformation could have taken place very well without the dissolution, or the dissolution without there being a Reformation. That this view is widely supported suggests that the 'top-down' historians are very much in the ascendancy in this aspect of Reformation studies.

Working on Chapter 4

Because the dissolution of the monasteries is as near to being a free-standing topic as you are likely to find on your course, it is worth being well-prepared to answer questions about it. This implies making a full set of notes.

Before proceeding further read the next section in this set of study guides. Having done this you should have identified the three issues around which it would be sensible to organise what you write. By far the simplest of these to tackle will be the 'What happened?' (the course) issue. Here you will need little more than a brief chronological outline of the major events between 1535 and 1540. The 'Why did it happen?' (the causes) and 'What were the effects?' (the consequences) issues will require rather more thought. You will probably find it easiest if you follow the pattern of the chapter in assembling your basic notes. However, it is important that you develop ideas of your own on these issues. The most foolproof way of ensuring that this is done is to include a 'What I think' heading in each of the second and third main sections of your notes.

Answering structured and essay questions on Chapter 4

When studying any event in history for examination purposes it is sensible to think explicitly about the three 'C's – causes, course and consequences – because this is how most question-setters tend to organise their own thoughts. Sometimes more than one of the elements features in a question, (especially where the event is relatively obscure and candidates cannot be expected to know a great deal about it). Look at the following structured question. How many of the 'C's are featured in it?

a) Explain the part played by Thomas Cromwell in the dissolution of the monasteries.
b) Why has the dissolution of the monasteries been so much criticised by historians?

Although part a) is mainly about the second of the 'C's, course, the use of the word 'explain' indicates that you should pay some attention to the reasons why Cromwell acted as he did. Remember to stress that there have been different interpretations about why Cromwell acted as he did.

However, by way of contrast, the norm with a main-line event such as the dissolution of the monasteries is for essay questions to focus on just one of the 'C's. The following selection will intentionally give the impression that one of the elements more frequently features in questions than the others. Which one is it?

1. What were the consequences of the dissolution of the monasteries?
2. 'The dissolution of the monasteries was a disaster for the common people of England.' How far do you agree with this judgement?
3. 'Henry VIII's attack on the monasteries was motivated purely by greed.' Discuss.
4. To what extent were the monasteries dissolved according to a preconceived plan?
5. Who gained and who lost as a result of the dissolution of the monasteries?
6. 'An act of state vandalism.' How justified is this description of the dissolution of the monasteries?
7. 'Henry VIII dissolved the monasteries because he wished to obtain their wealth. Their alleged spiritual and moral defects served only as an excuse.' How far do you agree with this point of view?
8. Discuss the statement that 'the dissolution of the monasteries sacrificed the spiritual interests of the many to the material interests of the few'?

Look at question 5. This is phrased in a very straightforward way and the examiner is therefore likely to be harsh on candidates who do not answer the whole question. Those who have not yet given much consideration to the historical concept of consequence ('effect' is another word used to describe the same idea) might imagine that the question only has two parts – about the gainers and about the losers. However, because it is the normal way of approaching the issue in historical study, the examiner's expectation will be that consequences are considered according to different timescales. Thus a distinction will need to be made between short-term effects and longer-term effects, suggesting an essay with four main sections (what are they?) as well as an introduction, which will explain why you have structured the essay as you have, and a conclusion.

The question appears to require a purely descriptive essay, and a very full answer containing a wide range of factual information will undoubtedly be given a good mark. However, it should be remembered that analytical writing (even when it is not explicitly demanded) is always likely to be more highly rewarded than a narrative or descriptive account. It is therefore advisable to make all essays analytical. In this case part of the analysis should be made apparent in the main body of the essay – by commenting on the relative extent and significance of the gains and losses that are being described – but there will almost certainly need to be a substantial concluding paragraph to pull the essay together. This should contain an assessment of whether or not the gains outweighed the losses. Would it be better to make one overall assessment or two separate ones – 'in the short term' and 'in the long term'? Whichever you decide, you will have a concluding paragraph which adds something to your essay rather than just summarising points you have already made. As no credit is given for repetition, this is an important point to remember in all essays you write.

Source-based questions on Chapter 4

1. The Commissioners and the Abbot of Glastonbury, 1539
Carefully read the extract from the Commissioners' letter to Thomas Cromwell, given on page 69. Answer the following questions.

a) Explain i) 'pardons' (line 5), ii) 'copies of bulls' (line 5) and iii) 'parcels of plate' (line 11). (*6 marks*)
b) What evidence does the extract contain that the Commissioners arrived at Glastonbury Abbey with the intention of gathering evidence to be used against the Abbot on a treason charge? (*6 marks*)
c) In what ways were the Commissioners successful in carrying out their intention? (*4 marks*)
d) Why did the Commissioners have this intention? (*4 marks*)

2. Thomas Cromwell's Annuity
Carefully read the extract from the annuity granted to Thomas Cromwell, given on page 72. Answer the following questions.

a) Comment on i) the size, and ii) the duration, of the annuity. (*4 marks*)
b) What could the abbot hope to gain by granting the annuity? (*3 marks*)
c) What does the grant imply about the personality and character of Thomas Cromwell? (*3 marks*)

3. The Complaint from Wembury
Carefully read the extract from the complaint about the Prior of Plympton found among Thomas Cromwell's papers (page 73). Answer the following questions.

a) What can be learned from the extract about the expectations that were held of a parish priest? (*5 marks*)
b) What two different types of 'property' did the Abbey of Plympton own in Wembury? Explain your answer. (*4 marks*)
c) What are the implications of the final sentence of the extract? (*4 marks*)
d) Who was the likely instigator of the complaint? Explain your answer. (*2 marks*)

4. The Injunctions to the Monasteries, 1535
Carefully read the extracts from the injunctions issued to religious houses during the visitation of 1535 (page 77). Answer the following questions.

a) What abuses might injunctions 4, 5 and 6 have been designed to bring to an end? Explain your answer. (*4 marks*)
b) Explain why many abbots might have thought that these injunctions were designed as a method of extorting money from them. (*4 marks*)
c) What evidence is there in the five injunctions quoted of an attempt to reform the monasteries in a Protestant direction? (*4 marks*)

d) What light do the injunctions throw on the government's intentions for the future of the monasteries? (*3 marks*)

5. The Dissolution of the Smaller Monasteries, 1536
Carefully read the extracts from the preamble of the act dissolving the smaller monasteries (page 78). Answer the following questions.

a) What justification is given for the dissolution of the smaller monasteries? (*2 marks*)
b) Why have historians concluded that this was mere propaganda? (*3 marks*)
c) What impression of the larger monasteries does this extract give? (*2 marks*)
d) What light does the extract throw on the government's intentions for the future of the monasteries? (*3 marks*)

6. Overview
Using information from all five extracts and your own knowledge comment on the view that 'the monasteries were dissolved because they were corrupt and had outlived their usefulness'. (*25 marks*)

5 A Move Towards Protestantism?

POINTS TO CONSIDER

For a long time historians have debated the extent to which England moved towards Protestantism during the last decade of Henry VIII's reign. In the process there has been much discussion about the roles of four people (Anne Boleyn, Thomas Cromwell, Archbishop Cranmer and Henry VIII). As you read this chapter for the first time try to do two things. Make up your own mind about the direction of religious policy between 1536 and 1547, and try to reach conclusions about the motives and the effects of the four characters.

KEY DATES

1514	Richard Hunne died by hanging. His case became the focus for anticlerical feelings
1525	William Tyndale's translation of the New Testament into English first published
1528	Simon Fish's, A Supplication for the Beggars, published
1536	Execution of Anne Boleyn; publication of the Ten Articles
1537	Bishops' Book published
1539	Act of Six Articles
1540 July	Fall of Thomas Cromwell
1543	King's Book published

Some readers will be surprised that thus far the book has been so much about politics and so little about religion. This balance of coverage is, of course, a reflection of the author's view that the Reformation during Henry VIII's reign was largely a political rather than a religious phenomenon (the 'top-down' interpretation). However, this is not to suggest that it had nothing to do with religion, which would be an untenable position to take. Not even the most extreme 'top-down' historians have argued in this way.

The question, therefore, is one of extent. There are two very distinct issues over which historians have disagreed for more than a generation: the extent to which the political (official) Reformation was made possible by religious factors, and the extent to which there was a religious as well as a political Reformation before 1547. Although no consensus on these matters has emerged so far, it is possible to detect the beginnings of a new orthodoxy. No doubt the disagreements will continue for some time, but the weight of research evidence is increasingly pointing in one direction. It is likely that the future will lie with those historians who maintain that the religious dimension of the Henrician Reformation was smaller than has often been thought and that, in 1547, England was in no sense irreversibly committed to religious change.

1 Religion and the Official Reformation

> **KEY ISSUES** What were the three elements of the old orthodox interpretation of the 'state' of the Church in England? Why was 1525 thought to be a crucial year in the English Reformation? What new interpretation has gone a long way towards replacing the old orthodoxy? What are the strengths and weaknesses of the revisionist interpretation?

a) The Old Orthodoxy

In the 1950s, 1960s and 1970s it was fashionable to argue that the official Reformation was merely the 'occasion' for the beginning of an inevitable process which, whether or not Henry VIII had needed a divorce or whether or not he had wished to make England 'an empire sufficient unto itself', would have resulted in the country discarding Catholicism and embracing Protestantism. In other words, it used to be maintained that a popular Reformation from below would have taken place whether or not there had been an official Reformation from above. This contention depended on several perceptions which remained the prevailing orthodoxy until the 1980s. The first of these was that there was widespread anticlericalism (dislike of the power which bishops and other clergymen exercised over people's everyday lives) in England in the decades before the break with Rome, resulting in the Catholic Church, as an institution, being highly unpopular among the population at large, and therefore ripe for replacement. Two examples were regularly quoted as being just the tip of the iceberg.

The most famous 'event' was the case of Richard Hunne who died by hanging in 1514 while in the Church's custody. Hunne was a prosperous Londoner who had taken on the Church authorities in the law courts because he felt that he was made to pay an exorbitant mortuary fee before his infant son could be buried. It was claimed by Hunne's supporters that the Church's response to this challenge had been to manufacture charges of heresy against their attacker, to arrest and murder him, and then spitefully to convict him of heresy posthumously so that his widow and children would be left destitute (one of the penalties for heresy was the loss of all property). The Church authorities' version of events was that Hunne was indeed a heretic and that he had committed suicide while awaiting trial. The affair remained a cause célèbre in the capital for many years and was regularly written and spoken about by those who wished to attack the supposed power or corruption of the Church.

The most notorious anticlerical publication was Simon Fish's, A Supplication for the Beggars (1528), in which he argued in lurid terms that all the country's economic ills were due to the greed, wealth and corruption of churchmen. In addition, he accused the clergy of gross immorality in that they:

1 apply themselves, by all the sleights they may, to have to do with every man's wife, every man's daughter and every man's maid that cuckoldry and bawdry should reign over all your subjects, that no man should know his own child ... Who is she that will set her hands to work to
5 get threepence a day and may have at least twenty pence a day to sleep an hour with a monk, a friar or a priest? What is he that would labour for a groat a day and may have at least twelve pence a day to be a bawd to a priest, a monk or a friar.

This 11-page pamphlet took the form of an address to the king requesting action. It has often been claimed (on scant evidence) that Anne Boleyn gave Henry a copy and that he secretly kept it in his possession for many months. The reader has normally been left to draw his own conclusion from this 'fact'.

The second vital perception was that the English Church was spiritually moribund by 1530. The claim was that its leading ranks were almost exclusively filled with royally-appointed absentees who often acted as unpaid (by the Crown) civil servants, and that serving parish priests were nearly all ex-peasants with minimal education and little sense of vocation – stretched to their limits in performing routine church services in a mumbo-jumbo fashion, and certainly unable to provide spiritual succour to their flocks. It was admitted that the English were still regarded as being one of the most 'religious' groups in Europe. However, it was maintained that this reputation was based on a widespread dedication to formal religious practices such as going on pilgrimages and lighting candles at altars, all of which were motivated by fear and superstition rather than by faith, belief or understanding. The implication was that this owed almost as little to true Christianity as did the pagan rights performed by the newly 'converted' indians of Central America.

The third 'plank' on which the contention depended was the existence of a body of fervent religious reformers who were willing and able to act as a catalyst for Protestant spiritual renewal among the population at large. Thus much was made of the existence of shadowy (but none-the-less real) groups of Lollards throughout the southern half of England, but especially in south Buckinghamshire and Coventry. Early sixteenth-century Lollards were third- and-fourth generation descendants of the original followers of John Wycliffe, a fourteenth-century English theologian whose teachings had long been held to be heretical. They therefore had every reason to keep themselves hidden from official view, a process assisted by the fact that most of them were artisans, who in the normal course of events would leave no mark in the historical record. As a result, our knowledge of them is almost entirely limited to the frustratingly brief listings of heresy trials.

Despite this, it seems reasonable to estimate that there were several thousand Lollards practising their reformed religion. At the heart of Lollardy was the study of the Bible in English, a hand-written copy of which was probably each group's most prized possession. This was in contrast to the official Church's activities which centred on the intervention of a priestly caste and of saints between the individual and Jesus. The majority of the population believed that saints could protect them in this life and ensure their well-being in the next.

If the Lollards were secretive, most other followers of a reformed religion were not. By 1530 contemporaries generally referred to them as Lutherans because they had all been influenced, to a greater or lesser extent, by the teachings of Martin Luther, whose writings had been circulating illegally in England for about a decade. But few deserved this description – as many of those who were charged with heresy strenuously protested – because the majority continued to believe in the central Catholic tenets of transubstantiation (the physical change of the bread and the wine into the flesh and blood of Jesus, in a repetition of his sacrifice on the cross, during the service called the Mass) and the existence of purgatory (the place where the souls of sinful, but not damned, people were painfully cleansed, often for many years, after death and before entry to heaven). What marked such people out as 'reformed' was the stress they laid on the reading of the Bible in a language they could understand.

For most of them this had to be English. Historians have agreed that a more correct label for them would be 'evangelicals' – meaning those who believe that the Bible is the place where God uniquely revealed himself to Man. Many of those who took up this position were vociferous in campaigning for a Bible in English to be legally available, and for preachers to be appointed to instruct the people in its correct interpretation. Because the Church authorities were generally suspicious of individuals who held these views (only a thin line divided moderate evangelicals from convictable heretics) many of them found themselves investigated on suspicion of heresy. Some were even so-charged and one or two were even convicted and punished with death in the years following the fall of Wolsey in 1529. In addition, there was the handful of self-proclaimed Lutherans who were prepared to die rather than to abandon their beliefs. Although all these people are known by name from the written records, it is impossible to quantify with any certainty those who believed similarly but escaped detection by the Church authorities. However, it is generally agreed that even by the mid-1530s they are most likely to have numbered hundreds rather than thousands. It is similarly agreed that, at this time, they were likely to fall into one of three categories: academics who were or had been at Cambridge University; members of élite (noble and near-noble families) who had often been influenced by individuals with a Cambridge background; and literate townspeople (primarily in London but also in the country's other ports, ranging from Newcastle to Bristol) for whom Lutheran literature was most readily accessible. The latter group was undoubtedly the most numerous, although it clearly lagged far behind the others in terms of influence.

One historian who argued that England was on the road towards a Protestant Reformation even before Henry VIII broke with Rome has nominated 1525 as the most important date in the English Reformation because William Tyndale's translation of the New Testament into English was first published in that year. The implication was that once the scriptures were free for all to read (or, for the illiterate majority, to have read to them) there was no way in which the onward march of Protestantism could have been halted – that, although the timing of the change was still in doubt, the final outcome was not. Tyndale was a remarkable man. He was an extraordinarily gifted linguist, speaking seven languages as if each was his native tongue, and was driven by an unquenchable sense of mission to provide his fellow countrymen with a version of the Bible they could understand:

> 1 I perceived ... how that it was impossible to establish the lay-people in any truth except the scripture were plainly laid before their eyes in their mother tongue ... For else, whatsoever truth is taught them, these enemies of all truth quench it again, partly with ... traditions of their
> 5 own making, founded without ground of scripture; and partly in juggling with the text, expounding it in such a sense as is impossible to gather of the text.

His absolute certainty about the task he had been placed on earth to perform, allied to a very pronounced meanness of spirit, meant that he was a merciless castigator of anyone who dared to disagree with him or to stand in his way. Once he had failed to win official blessing for his venture in England he moved to the Low Countries where it was easier to secure publication of sensitive material. But even here his mission was blocked and his translation was eventually produced in book form by a number of sympathetic printers in the Rhinelands. For the next 11 years he worked to improve his original translation (although most commentators judge that the effect of the changes he made was to turn a fine piece of scholarship into an increasingly partisan Lutheran publication), to discomfit his opponents by firing vitriolic broadsides of abuse in books and pamphlets (his running battle with Sir Thomas More is thought to have plumbed the depths of acrimonious debate), and to seek the support of Henry VIII for his endeavours (he ruined any chance he had by regularly issuing injudicious pronouncements). That he survived for so long in the Low Countries where the political climate was anti-Protestant was perhaps more surprising than the fact that he was eventually tried and executed as a heretic in 1536. By that time he had used up all the good will that even his powerful protectors could call on in his defence.

The claim that the England of 1530 was ripe for reformation has also been used to explain why Henry was able to implement the break with Rome and the establishment of the royal supremacy with so little opposition. The argument has been that the king acted with the passive acquiescence of most of his subjects, who were pleased that the Church for which they felt little love, and less respect, was having its wings clipped. The fact that most people barely raised one cheer for what was happening, rather than the three that might have been expected, has normally been explained in terms of apathy.

b) The Revisionist View

Beginning in the 1970s, a sequence of detailed studies has effectively undermined the old orthodox view. All three pillars of the interpretation have come under serious attack as a result of the efforts of the dozen or so research historians who have been notably involved in this work. The most prominent of these has probably been Christopher Haigh, both because of the quality and extent of his own original research and because he has taken the trouble to present a coherent view of the collective findings of these 'revisionist' historians. The claim that there was widespread and persistent anticlericalism in early sixteenth-century England has been discredited. This has not been done by arguing that the oft-quoted examples are invalid (they have been accepted as genuine), but by showing that they were exceptions to the rule rather than being the 'towering peaks' of it. Thus the picture that has emerged has been of a laity that was generally in harmony with its clerical counterparts, counting them and their activities as acceptable and often valuable parts of the order of things. The existence of frequently surfacing complaints about the Church's financial exactions has been likened to present-day attitudes towards the tax man – an easy target for abuse when people need to let off steam but otherwise thought of as carrying out a necessary function in society.

In addition, it has convincingly been claimed that most of the strongly felt anticlericalism that did exist was limited to two small groups of people which were well placed to have their views recorded in the surviving written records. London merchants, of whom Richard Hunne was a typical example, had long resented the way in which the Church authorities attempted to interfere with their activities (clerics tended to regard the pursuit of profit as verging on the immoral) and were vocal in their demands that they be answerable to the king's government alone. In this they were joined by the common law lawyers based in the London Inns of Court who traditionally resented the existence of a parallel legal system in which they were barred from practising. The Church courts were the preserve of a separate group of lawyers, the canon lawyers. Many London merchants and all members of the Inns of Court were highly educated and articulate. They were well versed in the techniques of drawing attention to their discontents. They did this with either a well-timed publication or a deputation to the king or one of his leading ministers. When parliament was in session they were particularly effective. Several dozen of them sat in the House of Commons (many boroughs were pleased to nominate Londoners to represent them as long as they promised to serve without the payment of expenses) and they were usually more confident and expert in public speaking than most of their 'country cousins'. It has been argued, for example, that the so-called anticlerical storm that swept the Commons in 1529 was totally of their making and might have attracted no more than the passing interest of historians had it not been for the fact that the Chronicle written by one of their number (Edward Hall) became one of the most readily available sources of information on the politics of the period.

Equally, it has been convincingly argued that during the opening decades of the century the Church was not at such a low ebb as had previously been assumed. Not only has it been shown that a number of long-serving bishops (besides the well-known John Fisher of Rochester) carried out their pastoral duties conscientiously and effectively, but it has also been made clear that in many dioceses with absentee post-holders very satisfactory arrangements were made for the bishop's duties to be carried out by a suitable deputy. Considerable evidence has also been gathered to suggest that the quality of the serving parish clergy was not generally as low as used to be thought. Although the records are too incomplete for a totally convincing case to be constructed, it appears that the priests who were denounced as being either incompetent or immoral (or both) were the exceptions rather than examples of the norm, and that most of the lower clergy gave satisfaction to those they served. While it cannot be claimed that many of them were well educated, knowledgeable about more than the central message of the New Testament, or able to preach sermons of their own composition, it seems reasonable to maintain that the large majority carried out their functions in a seemly manner and lived lives that attracted no scandal either to themselves or to their Church. In addition, numbers of them clearly displayed a very strong sense of spiritual purpose. Most of those known to us lived in the larger towns (religious enthusiasm in rural areas seems to have been rare) and were employed by groups of laymen, and some laywomen, who were formed into fraternities. Fraternities were not a new phenomenon, many having been in existence for centuries, but it appears that both their numbers and, in a significant proportion of cases, their zeal increased in the pre-Reformation period. It is true that some of them had always been, and remained, no more than élite clubs for the well-to-do, offering social recognition and insurance against an extended stay in purgatory (prayers were said and Masses were performed to benefit the souls of past members) to those who could afford to pay a high annual subscription. However, there is evidence that many attracted members because they offered a programme of activities whereby those who took their religion seriously could partake in prayer, worship, contemplation and discussion with like-minded people.

The growth in the number and size of spiritually dynamic fraternities has been used, along with scattered examples of individual lay people, such as Sir Thomas More and his daughter Margaret Roper, who made religion the cornerstone of their lives, to support the contention that there were many English people for whom the Catholic religion was much more than a series of mechanistic rituals. Although it has been impossible to quantify what was clearly no more than a tiny minority of the population, revisionist historians have felt justified in speculating that the number of those who wished to revitalize the Church from inside was at least of the same order of magnitude as those who wished to destroy what already existed and to replace it with Lutheranism. Thus, it has been possible for them to argue credibly (if not totally convincingly) that, had Henry VIII not brought about his politically inspired official Reformation, England would probably have remained within the Catholic fold and that a Protestant Reformation would not have taken place. Additional support for this admittedly unprovable hypothetical contention is provided by the fact that the majority of ordinary English men and women proved to be very reluctant to abandon their traditional religious practices, based as they might have been on fear and superstition, when they were eventually called upon to embrace a reformed, biblically-based religion in the decades following Henry VIII's death.

The cumulative effect of the work of the revisionist historians has been to cast doubt on the old orthodoxy that Henry VIII's political Reformation was made possible by the existence of widespread discontent over the exactions and shortcomings of the Catholic Church allied to a state of general apathy about its beliefs and teachings. Therefore, it is no longer safe to accept it as a 'historical truth'. It seems highly likely that the orthodoxy of the future will be that Henry VIII imposed his changes on a mildly resentful population which was generally content with things as they were and which saw no good reason why long-established traditions should be abandoned.

2 The Place of Religion in the Henrician Reformation

> **KEY ISSUE** In what ways have traditional and revisionist historians approached the study of the place of religion in the Henrician Reformation differently?

All historians writing on the topic since the middle of the twentieth century have agreed that there was much more to the Henrician Reformation than the divorce, the break with Rome, the royal supremacy and the dissolution of the monasteries. They have also generally agreed on what this 'much more' was. The disputes have been about the significance of the further changes and over the roles played by a variety of individuals in their introduction.

Those writers who have portrayed the Reformation in England as an event rather than a process have tended to tell a story that might fairly be summarised as follows:

(stage one) Henry VIII broke with Rome for political reasons, and spent the rest of his reign laying his hands on the wealth of the Church while attempting to prevent Protestants and their sympathisers from carrying his policies to their logical conclusions by radically reforming the country's religious beliefs and practices;
(stage two) by 1547 Protestantism had built up such a head of steam because of Henry's attempts to repress it that it burst forth in a virtually unstopable fashion once the king was dead;
(stage three) following the Edwardian Reformation which saw Protestantism firmly established, Mary was able to turn the clock back temporarily thanks in large part to her willingness to burn her opponents at the stake;
(stage four) the early years of Elizabeth I's reign saw Protestantism finally dominant and the inevitable process was complete.

Most revisionist historians view the English Reformation as a process rather than an event (see page 4). Therefore, they do not interpret individual happenings as further steps towards a known end or as parts of a coherent story. This explains why many recent writers have accorded incidents in the Henrician Reformation a different significance to that traditionally given them. When assessing the importance of each event they have tended to be more stringent in judging its effects. They have, for example, been less willing than has traditionally been the case almost to assume that each movement away from an orthodox Catholic position contributed to the eventual victory of Protestantism. They have demanded that the link between supposed cause and claimed effect be clearly demonstrated. The same has been the case when the actions of one person over a period of time have been assessed. The result of this difference of perspective has often been that both single events and the parts played by individuals have been given an alternative 'slant'.

a) Anne Boleyn

It used to be thought that Anne Boleyn was highly unpopular among

KEY ISSUES Was Anne Boleyn a Protestant? What was her effect on the Reformation in England?

the population as a whole partly because she was regarded as a whore who had ousted the rightful queen and partly because she was a Protestant. In recent decades the extent of both her unpopularity and of her Protestantism have been called into question as historians have been less willing to accept at face value the judgements made by contemporary observers. 'Anne of the Thousand Days' (so called because of the approximate time between her coronation in June 1533 and her execution in April 1536) was clearly very interested in religion and its reform. It has sometimes been implied that her involvement in religious matters stemmed entirely from self-interest, in that the more firmly established was England's break with Rome the more secure would be her position on the throne. This cynical view is definitely too extreme. Although there was certainly a selfish dimension to Anne's reasons for championing religious reform, there was also a deeply held personal belief. She was convinced of the benefits to be gained by lay people from studying the Bible and from having its meaning explained to them. She had been able to reach this conclusion from personal experience at a time when English versions of the Bible were outlawed because she was fluent in French and was breaking no law by possessing a New Testament in that language. But it is very doubtful whether she ever moved beyond this 'evangelical' position, and she seems to have held none of the Lutheran theological beliefs that would have justified the 'Protestant' label, as it was normally applied at the time, being attached to her. It seems that those contemporaries who accused her of Protestantism were either political opponents who were attempting to blacken her name, or religious conservatives who wished the Church to remain exactly as it was.

However, she was an activist. She shared with Henry a liking for religious debate and there is ample evidence, contained in third-party descriptions of dinner–table conversations, that the royal couple regularly discussed the Bible and its contents, and even that, in her enthusiasm, Anne frequently overstepped the mark by ignoring the established convention that the king should always be seen to have emerged victorious from any difference of opinion. Despite the rows or royal sulks that followed most such lapses, it does appear that Anne succeeded in persuading her partner that there was much to be gained and little to be lost by allowing his subjects to possess Bibles in

English, as long as the translation had received official blessing. Unfortunately for the cause she espoused, Henry was equally susceptible to persuasion by those who held the opposite point of view. Hence his support was very variable, and it was consequently left to others to capitalise on the groundwork that Anne had laid. But it seems that some of the queen's advocacy bore fruit during her lifetime. Although it has not been possible to prove direct cause and effect, it would be too much of a coincidence that all ten bishops appointed while she shared Henry's throne were reformers of whom she approved had she not played a significant part in their selection. And it has been possible to establish from surviving letters that the contemporary claim that she both supported and shielded Protestants, some of whom held unmistakably Lutheran views, was well-founded. Indeed she often seems to have taken the trouble to write to influential people at both home and abroad requesting either the appointment of reformers to clerical posts or the lenient treatment of individuals who were suspected of heresy. Such was the strength of the sixteenth-century patronage system that requests from a royal consort were normally treated as if they were instructions from the monarch himself. After all, for most people – at least in England – there was little sense in offending someone who might one day be in a position to harm you.

What was the cumulative effect of Anne Boleyn and her activities on the course of the English Reformation? In mid-1636 many of those who shared her religious outlook feared that it might be negative. It seemed as if her disgrace and Henry's despising of her might lead to a backlash in favour of those who were hostile to there being any reform of the Church. From the reformers' point of view Henry was distressingly liable to damn the cause as well as the individual who supported it whenever he fell out with somebody who was associated with a particular point of view. It was likely that his reasoning would be along the lines of, 'Anne Boleyn was in favour of religious reform; Anne Boleyn betrayed me; therefore religious reform is wrong.' In the event the backlash did not materialise. This was possibly partly because the other religious reformers who were close to the king – notably Thomas Cromwell and Thomas Cranmer – were able to distance themselves from the fallen queen at an early stage in the proceedings against her, and partly because the leading religious conservative – Anne Boleyn's uncle, the Duke of Norfolk – was implicated in the Boleyn disaster by family connection and was not in the position to capitalise on the reformers' discomfiture that he might otherwise have been. It was perhaps also because Henry did not brood for long over the wrongs that Anne Boleyn had supposedly done him. He was very soon head over heels in love again – with Jane Seymour whom he rapidly and lastingly (especially after she died as a result of giving birth to their only child) came to think of as the real love of his life.

However, if it is easy to agree that Anne did no damage to the Protestant cause, it is difficult to accept that her impact was of great significance. Despite the fact that 30 years later Protestant propagandists laboured to convince Elizabeth I that her mother had been a notable and direct contributor to the triumph of the anti-Catholic cause (a view still supported by some historians – a distinguished recent biographer has even claimed that she opened a door into England for Protestantism that it was subsequently impossible to close), it seems on balance reasonable to conclude that her long-term religious legacy was minimal and that she made it neither significantly more or less likely that England would eventually become a Protestant country.

b) Thomas Cromwell

> **KEY ISSUES** What were Cromwell's aims in matters of religion? What methods did he use? How successful was he in achieving his aims?

In July 1540 Thomas Cromwell, the architect of the break with Rome, the royal supremacy and the dissolution of the monasteries, was charged with being a Lutheran, was convicted, and was executed. For nearly six years he had been the king's vicegerent in religious affairs and had exerted the greatest day-to-day influence of any individual on the life of the Church. During this time the impact of the decisions he made and the actions he took was considerable and, some have argued, of lasting significance. Yet Cromwell maintained to the end that his beliefs always took second place to his loyalty to his master, and that he would have followed whatever religion he had been instructed to. It seems that within months of his minister's death Henry VIII was convinced of the truth of this claim, and most historians have subsequently come to the same conclusion.

However, this is not to suggest that Cromwell was not interested in religious issues for their own sake, because he clearly was. It is just that his first priority was always to prove his unswerving loyalty to Henry by carrying out whatever instructions he was given, even if these ran counter to either his policy objectives or his personal beliefs. Sufficient evidence exists for us to be able to identify Cromwell's religious preferences with a fair degree of certainty. The strategy he adopted in attempting to further his desired religious policies is also apparent. The result is that it is probably accurate to describe Cromwell as a moderate Lutheran who frequently attempted to use the fact that the king's attention was focused elsewhere to 'slip through' religious changes about which he knew his master would not have been enthusiastic had he been fully aware of what was happening. But, given his attitude towards Henry, he was always prepared to back-track or to take actions that were inconsistent with his previous decisions if this was necessary to satisfy the king's demands.

Cromwell utilised his position as vicegerent to the full. At the level of major policy, he attempted to manipulate the bishops as a group into devising detailed statements of belief that could be issued in the king's name and which would be binding on the entire Church. He also tried to secure their agreement to the publication of a Bible in English and to its distribution nationally. In addition, he issued several sets of highly detailed injunctions. His justification for doing this was that he was attempting to ensure that there was uniformity of beliefs and practices within the Church. These injunctions were instructions to those in positions of authority within the Church to ensure that certain practices ceased and that others were followed. In the process he – no doubt knowingly – gave the status of policy to numbers of practices that had never been agreed by either the king or any representative group of churchmen. He backed up his injunctions with circular letters to JPs instructing them to check that the bishops were carrying out their duties of enforcement vigorously, and to bishops to ensure that they monitored the effectiveness of JPs in reporting any failure to comply with his instructions. Given the inability of the central governments of most states at the time to arrange for their policies to be put into effect in the localities, Cromwell's record as vicegerent was remarkable. It was, of course, merely one facet of his outstanding administrative achievement as the king's chief minister.

1537 and 1538 were undoubtedly the years of Cromwell's greatest success in securing a movement away from the existing beliefs and practices of the Church of England. Some progress had already been made with, for example, the publication of the Ten Articles in 1536, a brief statement of the Church's beliefs which had been as significant for what it left out as for what it included. The Catholic Church practised seven sacraments (activities which, it was claimed, conferred God's grace on the participants or on those in whose names the sacrament was performed). Protestants argued that only those sacraments which had been authorised by Jesus, as reported in the New Testament, were valid. The Ten Articles included only these three sacraments (baptism, the Eucharist and penance): the other four were not rejected, they were merely 'lost'. Cromwell's plan seems to have been to follow up the Ten Articles with a much fuller explanation of what was to be believed and practised and what was not. His strategy was for this to be devised by a group of bishops and theologians under his tutelage and for the end product to be agreed by Henry 'on the nod'. The first part of the plan worked well and a draft text had been completed by the bishops after six-months' work in July 1537. One statement said to have been made by Cromwell to the bishops as they carried out their task is particularly revealing.

ı much less will he [the king] admit any articles or doctrine not contained
  in the scripture, but approved only by continuance of time and old
  custom, and by unwritten verities as you were wont to do.

Among other things, it showed Cromwell adopting the orthodox
Lutheran position that only those beliefs and practices that were
based directly on the authority of the Bible were justified. The
traditional Catholic view had been summarised very clearly by Sir
Thomas More during his running dispute with William Tyndale:

ı ... the gospel of Christ and the words of God that are now written in
  books, were all written in hearts before they were written in books,
  and yet were at that time of the same strength and authority that they
  be now. We say to Luther and Tyndale and all such other heretics, that
5 they say false in that they preach and teach, that men are bound to
  believe nothing but if it be written in books. So God is at his liberty to
  give his word in to his Church even yet at this day, by his own mouth,
  through the inspiration of his holy spirit sent there unto and by himself
  abiding ever therein and at the preaching of the Church, write it in the
10 hearts of the people's hearts at their preaching, at such time as it was
  yet unwritten in any of the apostles' books.

As perhaps Cromwell had hoped, Henry was too busy even to read the
draft document that was submitted for his approval. But he was too
shrewd a politician to allow the work to be published in his name
before he had scrutinised it carefully. He therefore instructed that the
book be clearly marked as carrying only the bishops' authority. Hence
when the Bishops' Book, as it was popularly known, appeared in
September 1537 it was not the definitive statement that Cromwell had
sought. In fact, it was not until 1543 that such a document was prepared. This was the King's Book, so-called because it had been vetted
in detail by Henry and reflected most of his conservative prejudices.

   Nevertheless, the reformers could count the publication of the
Bishops' Book as being another significant move in the right direction. This was despite the fact that, in some ways, it was a retreat from
the gains reflected in the Ten Articles. Thanks to the strong opposition to Cromwell mounted by a group of conservative bishops, the
four 'lost' sacraments were found and were included, although it was
explicitly stated that they were of lesser value than the other three.
But the document as a whole reads like a continuing slide away from
the orthodox Catholic position and towards Protestantism. This was
mainly as a result of the Bishops' Book's failure to confirm many traditional Catholic beliefs and practices – transubstantiation was not
mentioned, the Mass was largely glossed over, the special status of
priests was understated, and purgatory was only present by implication. Only a few clearly Protestant statements were made – such as
that the main duty of priests was preaching – presumably so as not to
alert the potential opposition to what was happening. In fact, the

The title page of Cromwell's Bible, generally known as the Great Bible, which was first published in 1539.

Detail from the title page of the Great Bible.

publication bore all the signs of being a step in the 'softening up' process that was such a typical and successful strategy of Cromwell's.

1537 also witnessed a more definite step towards Protestantism. It was ordained, thanks to the vicegerent's efforts, that within two years every parish church must possess a copy of the Bible in English and that it must be kept openly available for parishioners to read. Cromwell took upon himself the task of ensuring that the requisite number of Bibles was available. This involved him in almost as much work as it took to mount a military campaign, but he was determined to be successful, and he was. With hindsight, Protestant historians have felt able to judge this achievement to be one of the most significant in the whole story of the English Reformation. The argument has been two-pronged: that once the population as a whole was put in a position to find out what the Bible actually said the victory of Protestantism was assured, and that Cromwell's Bible (a translation by Miles Coverdale which was based substantially on William Tyndale's work), only slightly modified as the Authorised version 70 years later, became the cornerstone of an English Protestant literary and linguistic culture that survived nationwide well into the twentieth century and was thus massively influential. Revisionist historians have not been slow to challenge this verdict. They have convincingly maintained that the first argument is highly speculative and lacks solid evidence to support it, while the second argument does nothing to explain the success of Protestantism but rather is a result of that success.

In 1538 Cromwell published his second general set of Injunctions as vicegerent, following those issued to religious houses in 1535 (see page 66) and the first general set which had appeared in 1536. The Injunctions were detailed instructions to bishops about the policies they should implement in their dioceses. Whereas the orders given in 1536 had been rather vague (and therefore easy to ignore by those who did not welcome change), those of 1538 were much more specific and reformist in a Protestant direction. Instead of merely stipulating that superstitious practices should be discouraged, they stated that objects of dubious veneration, such as the relics of saints, should be removed from churches and that people should be actively discouraged from undertaking pilgrimages. Although many bishops dragged their feet over putting these policies into effect, not all did. Catholic sympathisers have written with great feeling about the cartloads of precious objects being transported to the Tower of London when the shrine to St Thomas Becket, one of the most famous pilgrimage sites in Europe, was removed from Canterbury Cathedral. One of the injunctions was subsequently of special significance to research historians in general and to genealogists in particular. This was the instruction that a register of births, marriages and deaths should be kept in every parish. The intention at the time was seemingly to ensure that evidence was available to decide whether a couple should be barred from marriage because of the closeness of their blood relationship, but the unintended consequence has been the accumulation of one of the richest sources of evidence for the study of family history.

However, even before Cromwell was executed in July 1540 the drift towards Protestantism had been reversed (see page 115), making it clear that it would have been very unlikely that he would have been able to manipulate Henry into a position of openly avowed Lutheranism however long he had remained in power. The little-by-little, 'slide' policy that was so effective when adopted by the monarch and the minister in concert could not be operated by Cromwell against Henry. Thus it appears justified to argue that Cromwell's strategy could have had little long-term effect on the struggle between Catholicism and Protestantism in England and that therefore his impact on the religious Reformation was doomed to be as temporary and potentially reversible as that of Anne Boleyn.

c) Thomas Cranmer

> **KEY ISSUES** In what ways was Thomas Cranmer a controversial figure? What was his effect on the Henrician Reformation?

For nearly 400 years Thomas Cranmer was one of the most controversial figures in sixteenth-century English history. Dozens of Catholic writers castigated him as the weak and changeable leader of the Church in England who, alone, had been in a position to save his country for Rome but who had been too cowardly to do so. In stark contrast, generations of defenders of the Protestant cause lauded him as one of their faith's foremost martyrs (he was burned at the stake during Queen Mary's reign). The hostile commentators generally had the best of the argument as no convincing justification was ever forthcoming for either Cranmer's rejection of the Pope's authority so soon after swearing, on taking up his duties as Archbishop of Canterbury in 1533, to obey him, or his attempt, as martyrdom beckoned, to reject Protestantism in a fruitless attempt to save his own life. However, in recent decades historians have become less and less interested in the sectarian battle and in the making of moral judgements – in deciding whether Cranmer was the champion of Protestantism or the betrayer of Catholicism and in determining whether his actions were right or wrong. Instead they have concentrated both on trying to explain how, although he was in a highly vulnerable position, he managed to survive throughout the Henrician Reformation while many others did not, and on assessing what influence he had on events between his surprise elevation in 1532 (see page 19) and Henry's death in 1547.

Of all the leading political figures of Henry's reign Thomas

Cranmer was perhaps the most 'human'. He was in no sense 'larger than life' and was certainly no hero. In many ways he was very ordinary. He began life with the advantage of being the son of a gentleman but with the disadvantage of being a younger son, who would have to make his own way in the world. However, his ambitions were very modest and he sought no more than a comfortable existence with no great stresses. Up to the age of 40 he managed this successfully, living most of his adult life as a relatively undistinguished member of staff at Cambridge University. Then a series of accidents shattered his peaceful existence. The skill with which he carried out a request to write in support of the king's divorce in 1529 brought him to the notice of Anne Boleyn. As a very junior, but seemingly very reliable, member of her faction, he was then persuaded to become the king's representative at the court of Charles V (a highly sensitive appointment at this juncture of affairs). On the long-awaited death of William Warham, the Archbishop of Canterbury, he was recalled to England and, to his and most other people's amazement, was asked by Henry to become the new Archbishop of Canterbury. It was made clear to him that refusal was not really an option.

The centuries-long running battle between Catholic and Protestant writers over Cranmer did much to cloud our understanding of his personality and character. Both the blackness and the whiteness of his many portrayals were equally unreal and essentially hid the true nature of the man. Perhaps the clearest appreciation of him can be gained by contrasting him with a contemporary such as Sir Thomas More. Both men held principles, but whereas More hung on to his with an unshakable grasp (even if that resulted in his own death), Cranmer followed his as far as his courage would allow (and certainly sometimes to his own disadvantage), but he could be pressured into abandoning them when the threat was great enough. Both men took life seriously but Cranmer lost little sleep over either the decisions he had to make or the actions he had already taken. He was able to rationalise away most of the guilt he might have felt. More was almost the opposite. He agonised over almost every decision, and was frequently filled with self-loathing over sins he suspected he had committed.

Their attitudes to their own sexuality were particularly revealing. Cranmer accepted his periodically strong sex drive as a natural occurrence and generally handled it with mature responsibility. As a young man he even resigned his comfortable position at Cambridge (where celibacy was the rule) in order to marry the woman with whom he had formed an attachment. In similar circumstances many men merely arranged to have a living-in housekeeper, but Cranmer's principles would not allow him to do this. As it turned out, his principles cost him little as his wife soon died and he was reinstated to his old position. While he was at Charles V's court in Germany he was persuaded by Lutherans that it was acceptable for a priest (as he by then was) to marry, and he took a second wife. On his return to England he found

Henry VIII taking a strong public line against such heretical practices. Cranmer admitted his 'fault' to his monarch, who allowed him to keep his partner with him as long as this was done in complete secrecy. For obvious reasons little evidence has survived about how this was achieved, although rumours did circulate about the Archbishop transporting a woman in a large box during the frequent moves of his household from residence to residence! However, it is known that Cranmer sent his wife out of the country in 1539 when it was explicitly made illegal for priests to continue living in a married state. Sir Thomas More believed that sexual desire was the work of the devil. He hated himself for allowing his lust for a woman to prevent him becoming a monk as a young man (he always believed that monasticism was his true vocation), and he customarily wore a hair shirt partly to subdue and partly to punish himself for his sexual desire. It was with some pride that he could claim that his second marriage had never been consummated.

Both men were highly intelligent (although More was clearly the only one with touches of genius) and both were excellent public speakers. But in private conversation they were poles apart. More could charm if he wanted to, but he could also be biting and sarcastic, especially to those of only limited intellect. Many people found him difficult to talk to. On the other hand, Cranmer is universally reported as being a pleasure to be with. He was always cheerful and friendly, never had an ill word to say about anybody, and had a self-effacing modesty of manner that placated the haughty and flattered those with lesser pretensions. He could speak his mind without giving offence and could diffuse the anger of others without causing them a loss of dignity. In modern parlance it would be said that his interpersonal skills were outstanding.

Many historians have identified this as one of the main reasons Cranmer was able to retain Henry's favour for so long. There is no doubt that the king liked him very much and was always predisposed to interpret what he said and did in the best of lights. This made it virtually impossible for those who wished to discredit the archbishop, because their views differed from his, to win Henry's sympathy. It seems that attempts to undermine Cranmer were always laughed at by the king. But there were other important reasons why the archbishop retained his monarch's confidence. Henry trusted him as far as he ever trusted anybody. He was confident not only that Cranmer would always do what he was told, whatever the circumstances, but also that he would never act independently in a manner of which his monarch would disapprove. It was Cranmer's lack of policy objectives of his own that probably set him apart from Cromwell in Henry's estimation. With Cranmer, Henry was confident that what you saw was what you got – there was no hidden agenda – whereas with Cromwell there was always the suspicion that there was something you were not being told.

Some writers have been tempted to dismiss Cranmer as nothing more than the king's yes-man. Such a verdict is misleading. It is correct that Cranmer's belief was that his loyalty to his king demanded that he accept whatever decisions Henry made and that he try his utmost to implement them, but he saw his duty as extending beyond this. He believed that he was called upon to offer his master the best advice he could at all times, even when he knew it was likely to be met with either disfavour or anger. Thus, for example, he pleaded with Henry not to allow Anne Boleyn's disgrace to damage the Reformation and he argued that leniency should be shown to Cromwell. The extent to which he was prepared to take his duty to advise fearlessly is recorded in the written response he made in 1538 to the more than 200 amendments Henry suggested be made to The Bishops' Book (see page 104) when he eventually found time to study it closely. Cranmer dealt with each point in detail and explained why most of Henry's proposals were either inappropriate or ill-founded. The fact that he took it upon himself to correct the king's grammar in places suggests much both about the archbishop and about his relationship with his master.

During the time Cranmer served Henry he was widely believed to be either a Lutheran or a Lutheran sympathiser. Although his views fluctuated over the period as the influences on him changed, (this inconsistency is partly what makes him so human), it is clear that he was always more of a Protestant than the king would have wished him to be. But, even more than Cromwell, he distinguished between his personal faith (which he openly declared to the king) and the policies he was helping to implement. Thus, at the extreme, he was prepared to pass judgements of heresy (leading to death by burning) on individuals whose beliefs were no different to his own when the king instructed him so to do. Those who have been revolted by such 'hypocrisy' have perhaps not thought deeply enough about what could lead a man to act in this way.

While the sectarian debate about Cranmer raged few writers were in any doubt that his influence on the Henrician Reformation was great, but a closer investigation of the facts suggests otherwise. If the question asked is, 'In what ways would the Henrician Reformation been different had Cranmer not been the Archbishop of Canterbury?', answers are difficult to find. In 1537–8 he supported Cromwell's attempts to move the theology of the Church towards Protestantism and in the years after 1543 he pursued a similar policy when invited to do so by the king. But his efforts were of no lasting significance, and one is really left with the highly intangible (and therefore essentially unquantifiable and unprovable) claim that his mere presence as the most senior cleric in the Church of England acted as an encouragement to those who wished to see Protestantism triumphant. Yet, however one argues the case, it is impossible to escape the conclusion that, although Cranmer's significance in the

Reformation after 1547 was very considerable, up to 1547 it was minimal in comparison to that of the man he served.

d) Henry VIII

> **KEY ISSUES** What pattern can be detected in Henry VIII's religious policy? Why does it make little sense to talk about Henry being either a Protestant or a Catholic?

The old orthodoxy that Henry VIII was a religious conservative who did all in his power to prevent any changes in the Church's beliefs or practices once the break with Rome had been made is no longer tenable. Detailed research (largely based on J.J. Scarisbrick's work) has shown that such a simplistic view cannot begin to reflect Henry's attitudes and actions with any degree of precision. In fact, such was the king's changeability, as new ideas were seized, enthused over and then dropped, that it has been impossible for recent historians to find any pattern that covers even most of the available evidence. For a time it seemed that a coherent explanation could be constructed by dividing the years 1533–47 into shorter periods and attaching an appropriate label to each one. Thus it was suggested that up to 1536 Henry was hostile to change, that in 1537 and 1538 he was prepared to countenance it in order to win the support of German Protestant princes for an alliance against Charles V, that between 1539 and 1543 he was very reactionary because he feared Protestant-inspired civil disturbance at home more than a Catholic-inspired invasion from abroad, and that after 1543 he became progressively more sympathetic to Protestant beliefs and that only his death prevented him from authorising significant changes away from Catholicism. But even this four-stage approach has proved to be too crude to fit the facts, although it still has its uses provided it is remembered that it is a way of identifying tendencies rather than a description of 'historical truth'. Possibly it is time to accept that any attempt to explain Henry VIII's policy towards religion during the last decade or so of his reign in terms of the Catholic–Protestant divide is doomed to founder in a sea of conflicting evidence that will prevent the emergence of generalisations that are both coherent and tenable. Perhaps modern writers' knowledge of the events of 1547–59 (when the Reformation became a 'fact') has led some of them to concentrate on asking the wrong questions of the earlier period (when Henry's concerns were mainly non-theological).

It has been when the attempt has been made to look at events from Henry VIII's point of view and with his perspective that clearer patterns have emerged. Then some consistency has become apparent. By 1533 the king had made up his mind – and his determination grew rather than diminished throughout the rest of his life – that he was going to be as much in control of the Church as he was of the rest of his kingdom. Thus the royal supremacy, as it emerged, was to be his (and his alone) as of right and was to be effective in practice rather than being the empty title that many of the higher clergy hoped and imagined it would be. Not only in the Act of Supremacy itself (see page 47) was Henry careful to ensure that this was so, but also in all the acts of parliament that followed and in all the authorised statements of policy that were published the message was the same.

No room for doubt was left that parliament's only role was to lay down the punishments to be inflicted on those who contravened the instructions given by Henry as God's direct and only representative as head of his Church in England and its associated domains. The same clarity of intention was apparent when it came to definitions of the role of the Supreme Head. Many churchmen assumed that the king, as a layman, would control the Church 'at arm's length', leaving decisions on matters of belief as well as all other areas of activity that had traditionally been the preserve of the priesthood to the ordained clergy. But they could not have been more wrong. Henry could find almost nothing that a priest could do that he, in his special God-given position, could not. He made it clear from the outset that the distinction between lay and clerical meant little to him. His intentions could not have been more starkly signalled than by his appointment of Thomas Cromwell as his vicegerent having control over the entire Church and being the superior of the highest clergyman, the Archbishop of Canterbury. Cromwell was a complete layman who had not even taken the minor 'orders' (making a man a member of the clergy, although not a priest) which for most people were an integral part of the formal educational system. Henry quickly established the fact that he himself would be the sole arbiter of religious belief. He was prepared to listen to the views of bishops and theologians and even to join with them in face-to-face debate on occasion. However, he was unprepared to delegate any decision-making powers on dogma to them. He even refused to accept the priesthood's claim to unique status as Jesus's spiritual heirs on earth. Their time-honoured argument was that they stood in an unbroken line of appointment from New Testament times, Jesus having ordained the disciples, the disciples having ordained the first bishops, and so on to the present. Henry argued that Christian princes would have been the ordainers (rather than bishops) from the outset had any existed at the time, and that there was therefore no reason why he should not ordain priests, or even carry out any of the other spiritual functions of the clergy, should he choose to do so. Fortunately, for peace within the Church, he was satisfied at receiving the agreement of the bishops that this was the position in theory. He generally chose not to test their loyalty by putting his more extreme claims into practice, although he did, for example, play the leading part in one heresy trial in 1538.

Another pattern is identifiable in Henry's dealing with religious matters, although it is made up of three inter-related strands and is therefore more complex. The first strand is his genuine interest in theology. Even as a young man he had been prepared to voice opinions of his own based on the relatively extensive study of the subject he had undertaken, and this had still been the case in his twenties when his defence of the Papacy against Martin Luther, which had resulted in the Pope granting him the title of 'Defender of the Faith', had been published. This interest, together with a growing (if not well-founded) belief in his expertise in the subject, remained throughout his life. However, he seems to have had little or no emotional commitment to the conclusions he reached from his studies and his discussions – they were held in his head rather than in his heart. It appears that he regarded the whole process as an elaborate intellectual game.

The opposite was the case with the second strand, his religious prejudices, which surfaced strongly from time to time and which he seems to have subjected to no searching intellectual scrutiny. They were 'gut-feelings' to which he reverted whenever he felt vulnerable or insecure. Their common feature was that they were very conservative. He believed that priests and others who had taken a vow of chastity should honour it for life. He was prepared to see them released from other vows (such as obedience to Rome) but he was unshakable in his determination that they should never be allowed to marry. Thus the nuns who were forced to leave their convents during the dissolution of the monasteries were barred from one of the routes to economic security that would have been open to some of them, and those priests (including Thomas Cranmer) who had married were required to set aside their wives in 1539. He refused to accept that lay people as well as priests should be able to take communion in both kinds (should be allowed to drink the wine – the blood of Christ – as well as eat the bread – the body of Christ – during Mass), he insisted that 'good works' (mainly religious observances rather than acts of charity) as well as faith were necessary for salvation, and he maintained an utter conviction in the existence of purgatory as the place where souls were cleansed before they could enter heaven. He also assumed the validity of transubstantiation and the benefits to be gained from confessing one's sins to a priest.

The third strand is easy to understand but difficult to chart in detail. Henry looked upon religious policy as a means to an end rather than as an end in itself. He thought of the Church as a pawn in the complex game of power politics, to be used to increase (or at least to maintain) his power at home and to further his designs abroad. Thus expediency rather than principle lay behind many of the decisions he made about the Church, its beliefs and its practices. The clearest examples of this are the dissolution of the monasteries, despite the fact that he supported much of what they stood for, the moves towards

Protestant beliefs made in 1537–8 in an effort to win German Lutheran support, and the preparations for the suppression of chantries made in the final years of his life. Chantries – sometimes specially built for the purpose, but more often side-chapels within existing churches – were the result of endowments made in rich people's wills so that Masses would be said in order to lessen the time their souls would need to spend in purgatory. Some of the endowments were so extensive that several full-time priests could be employed. There is no doubt that had Henry not died when he did the Chantries would have been swept away and their property would have passed to the Crown, despite the fact that the king still believed in the theology that underpinned their existence. (As it was, the Chantries' reprieve was very short-lived. They were swallowed up during the early months of Edward VI's reign.) Several other actions could equally well be used to illustrate Henry's religious pragmatism. Many historians have used the fact that the king ordered the almost simultaneous execution of a group of Catholics and a group of Protestants in 1540, indicating that he would not tolerate deviance of any kind, as an example of religion being used for overt political purposes. Similarly, the instruction of 1543 that the Bible should only be read by the well-to-do has been seen as having more to do with an imagined threat to public order than with any theological point of view.

These three strands were brought together in the Act of Six Articles in 1539. Henry indulged his love of theological debate by joining in much of the three-day discussion in the House of Lords about the measure, although the performance was really a sham because he had already decided what the outcome was to be. The beliefs and practices parliament was being used to support or to outlaw by specifying the punishments to be meted out to those who did not follow the Supreme Head's instructions. These coincided very neatly with Henry's prejudices. The six articles confirmed transubstantiation, private masses (for the living and the dead), and auricular confession, while banning the marriage of priests, the marriage of any others who had taken a vow of chastity, and the taking of communion in both kinds by lay people. The penalties laid down ranged from burning for denying the real presence (transubstantiation) to the loss of property and imprisonment during the king's pleasure for writing or speaking against or failing to comply with the other five. It seems fairly certain that the act was passed when it was in order to assure those who were alarmed by the drift towards Protestant beliefs and practices that there was no reason for them to take action over their worries. The fact that its passage led to the resignation of the two bishops popularly believed to be the most Protestant (Latimer and Shaxton) suggests that it might have served its purpose well.

Although these patterns can be used to make some sense of the part Henry VIII played in the religious life of the second half of his reign, it has to be admitted that they cannot give coherence to the whole story. But that is because nothing can. Henry was an erratic, impulsive and complex man who was skilled at confusing those around him about what his conscious motives were. In addition, it is doubtful whether he possessed sufficient self-awareness even to understand at any depth himself why he did things. Thus the historian must often be satisfied (if not pleased) with establishing partial explanations that seem to ring true.

If, in a historian's timeshift dream, Henry could be asked whether he was more a Catholic or more a Protestant he would probably argue that the question was meaningless because he did not think of religion in these terms. He viewed those who passionately espoused either cause as a threat to be eliminated. This was not, as has sometimes been implied, because he could not make up his mind which of the two possible choices to select. It was because he claimed that these were not the only possibilities. Although his religious aspirations were never spelled out (and probably never existed) in a fully developed form, sufficient evidence exists for a good impression of them to be gained. Henry saw the future of Christianity as lying in a series of independent Churches each of which was ruled over by a prince, who would lay down its organisation, beliefs and practices as he felt he was instructed to do by God. Thus the one (invisible) Church of God would take its earthly (visible) form as a collection of free-standing units which differed in detail but which were all equally valid. Hence, in 1538, he terminated his efforts to reach an agreement with the Lutheran princes of Germany when it became clear that they required him openly to accept their joint statement of belief (the Confession of Augsburg). His response was that he was quite capable of deciding such issues for himself without the help of foreigners. He rejected the implication that you had to be either a Protestant or a Catholic.

Although the large majority of the ten thousand or so of the king's subjects who made up the 'political nation' seem to have tacitly agreed with this perception, a significant minority of them held strong views about the beliefs and practices they wanted Henry to lay down for the English Church. For the 'conservatives' the hope was that long-established religious traditions would be maintained. They were particularly attached to the sacraments, especially the Eucharist with its miracle of transubstantiation, and to the cluster of beliefs and practices associated with the efficacy of good works in securing salvation. These included the possibility of others (priests, saints and especially the Virgin Mary) intervening with Jesus on the individual believer's behalf, be he alive or dead and in purgatory. Few of them had any real desire to see the Pope re-established as the Head of the Church and it is therefore possibly misleading to refer to them as Catholics. The 'reformers' were mainly evangelicals who looked upon the Bible as the main (for some it was the only) legitimate source of knowledge about God's revelation to Mankind. Most of them therefore wished the Church of England to require its members to accept no beliefs and to perform no practices that were not directly based on biblical authority. As a consequence, they rejected much of what the conservatives valued most highly. The gap between the two groups was enormous.

Much as Henry regretted the existence of this situation – his view was that loyal subjects should leave such issues to be decided by their prince and should meekly accept his decisions, whatever they might be – he was realistic enough to recognise that it was likely to continue.

His strategy for dealing with it appears to have been relatively consistent. He sought to punish those who held either extreme conservative (papist) or extreme reformist (Lutheran) views, while holding out hope to the moderates in both groups that royal decisions might favour them in the long term. Presumably, the intention was to minimise the risk of any group being driven by despair to resort to armed insurrection. This approach was most noticeable in the 1540s, after Cromwell's fall, when a conscious effort was made to balance the numbers of 'conservatives' and 'reformers' in positions of power, for example as members of the Privy Council. This 'even-handed' way of working has provided historians with ample evidence to construct a case either that Henry moved the country towards Protestantism or that he attempted to hold it true to the essentials of its Catholic past. There is therefore plenty of scope for the thoughtful student to form an independent judgement about both Henry VIII's aims in his religious policy and the effects of the action he took.

Summary Diagram
A Move Towards Protestantism?

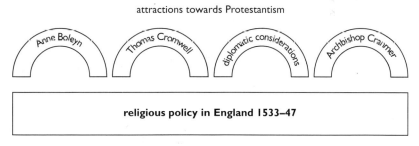

attractions towards Protestantism

Anne Boleyn

Thomas Cromwell

diplomatic considerations

Archbishop Cranmer

religious policy in England 1533–47

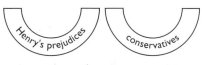

Henry's prejudices

conservatives

attractions towards Catholicism

Working on Chapter 5

The two main sections of this chapter deal with quite separate issues, and thus you will need to prepare what are effectively two sets of notes. However, the approach in each case can be the same.

Because the chapter takes the form of two very analytical discussions, your notes will need to be different from those you make from narrative or descriptive material. The best way to ensure that you understand each of the discussions is to note down the 'flow of ideas' presented. The most effective method of doing this is to summarise the point being made in each paragraph. Do this as briefly as possible. A phrase or short sentence should be sufficient in every case. As you are concentrating on ideas, no facts should be included.

Your second task is to note the key facts. You might be surprised to find how few of these there are. Your reason for doing this (and for subsequently memorising what you write) is so that you will be able to use the facts in different combinations when answering questions other than those tackled directly in the chapter. As I expect you already understand, knowing the facts is not sufficient at this level of study. What really matters is how you can use them.

Answering structured and essay questions on Chapter 5

It is relatively unusual for essay questions to be set that could be answered from this chapter alone. It is much more likely that you would be expected to combine material from several chapters (and perhaps even from other books as well) in planning your answer. Decide which of the following questions would require knowledge of issues and events in addition to those covered in this book.

1. To what extent had England become a Protestant country by 1547?
2. Did Thomas Cromwell or Thomas Cranmer have the greater effect on the English Reformation?
3. What were Henry VIII's motives in his dealings with religious issues?
4. Would you agree that 'the most significant event in the spread of Protestantism in England was the publication of the Bible in English in 1538'?
5. How far was Henry VIII in charge of the Henrician Reformation?
6. Why have the 1530s been regarded as one of the most revolutionary decades in English history?
7. Is it true that Henry VIII wished England 'to remain Catholic but without the Pope'?

Look at question 1. It contains a phrase that will need to be defined explicitly before the question can be answered directly. What is the phrase? Where would be the best place in the essay to give your definition of it? The definition will need to have two major components.

If the first is 'what the population as a whole believed and practised', what will the second be?

An answer to question 3 could be made up of a collection of points, each explaining and illustrating a different motive, and presented in a random order. However, this would result in the essay lacking 'shape' and a clear sense of direction. These faults could be avoided if, at the planning stage, the motives chosen for discussion were formed into several groups according to features they have in common. If one of the groups were to be made up of motives relating to Henry's desire to make himself more powerful, what other general motives might be used as labels for groups? You would need to describe the chosen groupings for his motives in the introductory paragraph of your essay. What purpose would the concluding paragraph serve in such an answer?

Source-based questions on Chapter 5

1. Anticlericalism
Carefully read the extract from Simon Fish's A Supplication for the Beggars on page 93. Answer the following questions.

a) What accusations are being made against the clergy? (*3 marks*)
b) What evidence does the extract contain to suggest that the author was not an impartial observer? Use quotes in your answer. (*4 marks*)
c) In what ways have historians differed in their opinions about the significance of publications such as Simon Fish's pamphlet? (*3 marks*)

2. William Tyndale
Carefully read the extract from William Tyndale's explanation of the importance of the Bible being available in English, given on page 95. Answer the following questions.

a) Who were 'these enemies of all truth' (line 4)? (*2 marks*)
b) Explain the two ways in which, Tyndale claimed, they quenched the truth. (*6 marks*)
c) Describe the tone of the extract. (*2 marks*)
d) What evidence does the extract contain that it was written by a Protestant? Use quotes in your answer. (*5 marks*)

3. Sources of God's Word
Carefully read the statement that Thomas Cromwell was claimed to have made to the bishops working to prepare a statement of the Church of England's teachings (page 104) and the extract from Thomas More's writings (page 104). Answer the following questions.

a) What was Cromwell attempting to do by speaking as he did? (*3 marks*)
b) Was Cromwell justified in representing this viewpoint as being the king's? Explain your answer. (*3 marks*)

c) Explain the differences between Cromwell's and More's views about the sources of God's word. (*4 marks*)

d) What were the implications of these differences? (*5 marks*)

4. The Title Page of the Great Bible

Carefully study the illustrations of the title page of the Great Bible which are reproduced on pages 105 and 106. Answer the following questions.

a) Describe the sequence of events portrayed in the illustration. (*6 marks*)

b) In what ways was the artist attempting to flatter Henry VIII? (*3 marks*)

c) Comment on the wording of the second paragraph of the text in the centre of the page which reads, 'Oversene and perused at the comandment of the kynges hyghnes, by the ryghte reverende fathers in God Cuthbert bysshop of Duresme, and Nicolas bisshop of Rochester.' (*6 marks*)

d) What evidence does the illustration contain to suggest that the publication of the Great Bible marked a move towards Protestantism in England? (*5 marks*)

6 A Henrician Reformation?

Many historians have employed the term 'Henrician Reformation' to describe the events discussed in the four previous chapters. Others have chosen to avoid using the label because they consider that it carries with it major assumptions, some of which are misleading if not downright inaccurate. This difference of opinion is important but, unfortunately, it is not easy to resolve, as the argument involves issues and contentions that are unprovable one way or the other. It is therefore necessary for each person to decide for him or herself how far the term is valid. The task is difficult, but one result of carrying it out is likely to be the acquisition of a much more precise understanding of the nature of the changes that took place in organised religion in England in the second half of Henry VIII's reign, and of the causes and consequences of what happened.

One of the reasons why the phrase has caused unease is because of the sense of coherence that its use gives to the collection of events that fall within its meaning. This has frequently been part of a general suspicion of any grouping and labelling of facts that historians have carried out a long time after the events in question took place, especially if the terms invented include words such as 'rise', 'revolution' or 'reformation'. In the study of sixteenth-century English history, for example, concepts such as 'the rise of the gentry', 'the rise of capitalism' and 'the revolution in government' were all first thought of in the twentieth century (as was 'the Henrician Reformation') and have provoked profound disagreements among historians over a long period. The feeling has been that it is too easy for researchers in good faith to perceive patterns that exist only in their own minds and then to gather together evidence to support the hypotheses they have already developed. Some would argue that 'the Henrician Reformation' is one such case.

Another reason why such terms are often mistrusted is because it is felt that historians, by organising their studies according to them, separate some events from other happenings alongside which it is believed they ought to be considered if their true historical significance is to be appreciated. The contention is that the use of concepts such as 'the Henrician Reformation' results in the events that are thought to fall within its boundaries being studied separately from other contemporary events that would provide the context within which the changes affecting, in this case, religion could be most fully understood. This view taken to its logical conclusion, as it has been by some French historians, ends up in a theory of historical studies which maintains that a meaningful understanding of the past can only be gained by studying all aspects of life at one moment in time, and that all less wide-ranging investigations are doomed to be so far from the 'reality' of the period being researched that they have little value.

The two reservations explained above are 'generic' (relating to the use of such terms in any situation). Other causes of concern have been specific to the term 'the Henrician Reformation' itself. It is the word 'reformation' that has been seen as problematic by some commentators, who have been worried about the ideas that are associated with it in most people's minds. The first of these associations is with Protestantism. This results from the word 'reformation' almost always being used in writings about the early sixteenth century to mean the replacement of Catholicism by some form of religion with reformed beliefs and practices. But not everybody would agree that this is what was happening (or even beginning to happen) in England during Henry VIII's reign, and the fear is that the mere use of the phrase 'the Henrician Reformation' will imply that it was. The second association is with the reformation that occurred during the reigns of Henry's children. The feeling has been that by describing the events of 1533 to 1547 as 'the Henrician Reformation' the assumption is being made that these happenings formed the first stage of the process normally described as 'the English Reformation'. The argument is that the case needs to be proved and not merely to be assumed, as for so long it was in the political histories written about the period. The third association is with the reformation that was simultaneously taking place in parts of Germany, Switzerland and Scandinavia and which was mostly based on the teachings of Martin Luther. It has been thought that the use of the term 'the Henrician Reformation' will cause many people to assume that what was happening in England was a part of the wider European movement against the powers of the Papacy and the teachings of the Church that was headed by the Pope. For those who maintain that what was done under Henry VIII's authority was only coincidentally related to the European reformation and that England's break with Rome and its associated events would have taken place whether or not Martin Luther had ever lived, this association of ideas is most misleading.

Persuasive as the arguments might seem, only a very small minority of English-speaking historians would object to the use of the term 'the Henrician Reformation' on the basis of the generic arguments. This is largely a result of such reasoning being outside the generally accepted tradition of historical research in Britain. Because of the danger of misleading associations, more might be willing to question the wisdom of inventing such a phrase if it did not already exist, but as it is already in general use the majority opinion would undoubtedly be that it is a helpful concept to have provided its users are aware of exactly what they mean by it. Thus for most historians the initial answer to the question, 'Was there a Henrician Reformation?' would be, 'It all depends on how the term is defined.'

The success of Dickens and of the revisionist historians in establishing the case for studying the beliefs and practices of the population as a whole means that any definition of 'the Henrician

Reformation' that did not include the 'popular' reformation would be regarded as deficient. But there the unity of those historians who favour a 'bottom-up' approach would end. Dickens and his supporters would contend that the reign of Henry VIII witnessed a sufficient spread of Protestant beliefs in England that, given the weakness of the Catholic Church, it was almost inconceivable that reformed ideas would subsequently be eradicated or that Protestantism would fail to win over almost the entire population within a generation or two. They would therefore argue that the term is an accurate description of what took place and they would be content for its use to carry with it the three main associations that some others have considered to be a cause for concern. They would have no doubts about the extent of the changes in many people's beliefs or about the fact that thousands of individuals adapted their religious practices, as far as they could without inviting persecution, to match their new faith. They would support their claim by pointing to the apparent rise in Bible study among the élites nationwide and among almost all classes in the larger towns, and by drawing attention to the seeming decline in activities that were motivated by a desire to earn 'merit' or to result in the intercession of a saint on one's behalf (going on pilgrimages, and leaving money in wills to existing shrines or for the establishment of new ones). Thus they would view the changes in popular religion that took place in the period 1520 to 1547 (the significance of the earlier date being that the changes were well under way before Henry VIII began his 'official' Reformation) as being an integral part of the English Reformation that led to the country abandoning Catholicism in favour of Protestantism. They would also stress that Lutheranism was the major influence on most reformers (hence the link with the continental Reformation) and that it was the import of books and pamphlets from Germany that continually added fuel to the movement favouring religious change. However, they would not rest their case there. Dickens explicitly stated that what he was seeking was a balance between 'bottom-up' and 'top-down' approaches, not the replacement of the latter by the former. Therefore the actions of central government would form a significant part of any definition of 'the Henrician Reformation' by this group.

Revisionist historians would probably prefer it if the term were not to be used, as they would reject any definition of it that would be accepted by the supporters of the old orthodoxy. They would claim that the case for there having been a 'popular' reformation before 1547 remains unproved and that the evidence advanced to support the contention does no more than show that there were a few dozen active Lutherans who are known by name and probably a few hundred further anonymous supporters whose existence can reasonably be inferred from the written records. But they would disagree with Dickens that these people were the tip of a Protestant iceberg. In fact, they would argue that Lutherans formed a minute, generally forlorn and vulnerable minority which was mistrusted by Henry VIII, by most of the Church hierarchy and by the population as a whole, and which would have disappeared almost without trace had official encouragement and protection not been forthcoming during Edward VI's reign. In addition, they would maintain that the 'official' reformation carried out by Henry VIII with the blessing of parliament was of minimal significance in the religious history of the period. Their criterion for assessment would be the effect of the changes on the religious beliefs and practices of ordinary people, and they would be confident of being able to show that these were small in scale and limited in geographic extent. They would accept that there were changes in a few places – mainly in the larger towns within dioceses with a reformist bishop – but would maintain that what little evidence there is suggests that the divorce, the break with Rome, the royal supremacy and the dissolution of the monasteries had virtually no impact on popular religion, while the directives on beliefs and practices issued after 1536 were ignored almost everywhere if change was sought.

The 'top-down' historians, who have tended to concentrate their attention on the actions of Henry VIII and his government, have generally accepted the use of the term 'the Henrician Reformation' without demur. For them the changes brought about by the legislation of 1533–6 (the break with Rome and the royal supremacy) were sufficient in themselves to warrant the use of the disputed term. They would claim that these jurisdictional changes, although having more to do with politics than religion, had such an effect on the Church in England and were so clearly a part of a single process that it is justifiable to describe them collectively by using a phrase which indicates that something of major importance took place. Their argument would be based on the dramatic diminution in the power and status of the Church that resulted from Henry's actions. They would contrast the situation before 1530 with that after 1536: the difference between a free-standing institution (a state within a state – albeit one that was clearly inferior to the lay power), with its own independent legal system and owing its final allegiance to a foreign potentate, and an organisation which was clearly no more than a branch of the state, with all its activities likely to be interfered with by the monarch or somebody acting on his behalf. They would draw particular attention to the way in which the prestige of the Church's hierarchy declined with bishops and mitred abbots (the heads of the richest religious houses) no longer being generally regarded as the equals of the lay peers, and with the Church losing its majority in the House of Lords once the monasteries were dissolved.

Thus even those followers of the old orthodoxy, that Henry altered the structure of power within the Church and the balance of power between the clerical and lay estates while successfully managing to resist change in religious beliefs and practices, would have a powerful case to advance. Those who maintain that, in addition to the political reformation which he supervised, Henry VIII also initiated doctrinal changes away from Catholicism would have a yet more persuasive argument to put forward. They would be able to claim that 'the Henrician Reformation' was a reformation 'in the round', although it was initiated totally from the centre.

Some writers have argued forcefully that during the last two or three years of his life Henry was actively moving the Church of England towards Protestantism. They have presented a picture of an aging monarch who fell increasingly under the influence of his wife, Catherine Parr, who was a Protestant in all but name, and of leading members of his household who were of a similar persuasion. Further explanation of the king's motives has been given by claiming that Henry became increasingly concerned that his death would be followed by a Catholic backlash, resulting in the rescinding of the measures by which he had strengthened the State at the expense of the Church and in a renewal of the subservience to Rome. It has also been argued that this worry led him to tilt the balance of the Church away from Catholicism in order to prevent his fears from being turned into reality. However, the evidence that has been brought forward to substantiate this interpretation has been somewhat scrappy. There has been the negative evidence of what Henry did not do. He did not follow up the pro-Catholic doctrinal definitions of 1543 (the King's Book and the limiting of those who were to be allowed to read the Bible in English) with a concerted attack on reformers, as he had done in 1539 after the passage of the Act of the Six Articles, when hundreds of Londoners had been arrested on suspicion of being heretics. Nor did he prevent Catherine Parr from ensuring that his two younger children (Edward and Elizabeth) were taught Protestant beliefs, or object to Thomas Cranmer bringing his wife back from Germany.

If this indirect evidence is unconvincing, it has to be said that the direct evidence is hardly persuasive. In 1544 Henry ordered that the Litany (a part of the normal Church service in which the priest and the congregation took it in turns to make requests of God according to a set formula) be in English rather than in Latin. This was a step in the direction of the Protestant position that acts of worship should be performed in a language that the participants understood, and the process was taken a stage further when an English translation of all Church services was published in 1545. However, as priests were not obliged to use it, its impact was fairly limited. Potentially rather more telling was Henry's suggestion, made six months before his death, that the kings of England and France should jointly reject both the Mass and whatever remained of papal authority within their domains. It has been the proposal to abandon the Mass that has been considered to be so significant by those historians who have argued that Henry made a late shift towards Protestantism, (the Pope's powers in England were by then non-existent), because it had been Henry's previous insistence of retaining the centrality of the service in the Church's devotional life that had become symbolic of his conservatism in doctrinal matters. Unfortunately for those who wish to read a large amount into this incident it seems that the suggestion, which was reported as being made to the French ambassador, was no more than one of Henry's irresponsible 'kite-flyings' (of which there were many) and did not result from any carefully thought out change of policy.

A second of the mainstays of Henry's commitment to Catholic beliefs and practices was his support of traditional attitudes towards purgatory and the steps that could be taken to shorten the time that souls suffered there. Therefore his clearly signalled intention to do away with chantries and their priests (see page 114), whose main purpose was to pray for the souls of the dead, was bound to be seen by contemporaries as a weakening of official support for the theology that underpinned their existence. However, it seems that this was a purely incidental effect. There can be little doubt that Henry's motives for wishing to destroy the chantries had to do with greed rather than theology, and that (as with the dissolution of the monasteries) it would be dangerous to read too much significance for religious policy into an action that was almost entirely a matter of the Crown's search for additional wealth.

It might be appropriate for the same warning to be issued about the eclipse of the Catholic faction at Court during the final months of Henry's life, when the group's two leading figures were disgraced. It appears that Stephen Gardiner was instructed to take up residence in his bishopric of Winchester because he raised objections to the king's proposal to exchange Crown land for estates owned by the see of Winchester. Such exchanges, which were always markedly to the Crown's advantage, had become commonplace during the previous decade or so and were Henry's way of laying his hands on parts of the Church's wealth that he could not acquire more directly. Gardiner was exceptional in being brave (or foolhardy) enough to attempt to place difficulties in the king's way. The Duke of Norfolk was awaiting execution in the Tower of London when Henry died not because he was a leading opponent of moves towards Protestantism but because he was the father of the Earl of Surrey, whose arrogant assertions about his descent from the kings of medieval England had led to his conviction of high treason and subsequent beheading. The claim that these events were connected and that they help to prove that Henry was clearing the way for a public acceptance of Protestantism seems to be unfounded. The evidence is certainly not conclusive one way or the other but, on balance, it appears more likely that the king's intentions after 1543 were the same as they had been in the previous years. He was attempting to retain the loyalty of both those who wished to see no changes in the Church's teachings and practices and those who wished to see moves towards Protestantism. His strategy was to show sufficient favour to each side in turn to give its members hope of ultimate victory.

So what conclusion should be reached about whether or not there was a Henrician Reformation? It is certain that any answer will need to be prefaced by a clear definition of what the term is being taken to mean. Even once this has been done, it appears that there is no definitive answer to be given. Too many unresolved disagreements exist for this to be possible. Therefore, the use of qualifying words such as 'probably' and 'possibly' will be very necessary. This is not to argue for wishy-washy woollyheadedness. It is merely to suggest that the historian's task is sometimes as much to do with admitting the limitations of his or her knowledge (because of the nature and the extent of the available evidence and of the inquiry being undertaken) as it is to do with stating clear-cut findings. For many people – and certainly for me – one of the perennial attractions of the subject is that little is written on tablets of stone and that there is always the hope of learning more and the likelihood of tentative conclusions needing to be modified in the light of fresh evidence. For those who crave certainty (or at least the appearance of it) History will be a frustrating subject to study. But for those who enjoy combining factual knowledge about people and events with creative thinking about concepts and issues the fascination is likely to be strong and lasting. Henry VIII may be dead and buried but the controversy surrounding him lives on and on.

Summary Diagram
A Henrician Reformation?

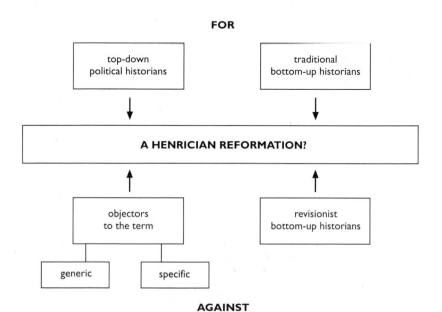

Working on Chapter 6

It is probable that you will only get as much out of this concluding chapter as you are able to put into it. One quick reading is likely to leave you with little more than a realisation that there are no simple answers. A second, slower, and more thoughtful reading will be needed if you are to put yourself in a position where you can gain anything of significance.

During your second reading stop at the end of each of the chapter's 14 paragraphs and write a one-sentence summary of the main point being made. When you have completed your set of 14 sentences read it carefully to ensure that you understand which groups of historians would i) support, and ii) not support, the use of the term 'the Henrician Reformation' and why. This is the factual information you need to extract from the chapter.

Once that has been done you will be in a good position to begin the much more difficult but vital work of identifying issues and deciding your point of view about them. Using your summary, make a list of the issues over which historians have disagreed. These should fall into three groups, which could be headed 'the nature of historical study', 'the nature of the English Reformation' and 'differing interpretations of what happened in Henry VIII's reign'. You may have already decided where you stand on some of these issues. Some you will probably never have considered before. Now is the time to think each one through as far as you can and to reach a provisional conclusion about it. Do not be surprised if sometimes your verdict is 'undecided'. It would be unrealistic to expect to be able to take up a clear-cut stance on every point. For example, you have not been provided with sufficient evidence to do so in some cases. What is important is that on issues over which you do decide to sit on the fence you are able to outline the relative strengths and weaknesses of the conflicting points of view, and to explain why you are keeping your options open. Remember that reasoned indecision is much to be preferred (especially by examiners) over unwarranted certainty. A carefully explained 'I'm not sure' is often a sign of strength rather than of weakness.

Hopefully you will now feel that you have taken what this book has to offer. However, there is one more task to be undertaken before you can consider your work to be complete. You need to relate what you have learned from this book to the general issues you have been studying about Henry VIII and his reign. If you followed the advice given at the end of chapter 1, you will now be in a good position to reach your own conclusions about Henry VIII's personality and character. If you have done what was suggested in the 'Working on ...' sections at the end of chapters 2–5 you should be able to do the same in relation to Henry's aims and methods and the issue of how far he controlled or was controlled by his leading ministers. Once all this has been done, you should be in a strong position, with an appropriate fund of factual knowledge and ideas at your disposal, to tackle whatever questions an examiner chooses to set before you. Better still in the long run, although you may not agree with this order of priorities at the moment, you will have further developed patterns of thought that you will find useful in most aspects of life.

Further Reading

1 The English Reformation

If you are studying this topic at degree level it would probably be most helpful if you next looked at Richard Rex, *Henry VIII and the English Reformation* (Macmillan 1993) in the British History in Perspective series.

In particular, the bibliography offers reliable guidance on where to start any detailed research you will be doing.

Those who wish to study the Reformation in England as a complete topic at a level below degree level would be well advised to start by reading chapters 5 and 6 of Rosemary O'Day, *The Debate on the English Reformation* (Methuen 1986) which will allow the books listed below to be placed in a clear historiographical context and make it more likely that the interpretations they advance will be recognised and evaluated rather than just being accepted. Only then will it be possible to extract the maximum benefit from reading as much as possible of the standard work on the topic: A.G. Dickens, *The English Reformation* (Batsford 1964 – second edition 1989).

It is vital to ensure that the second edition is used as the changes from the first edition are both numerous and significant. This book has been so influential that it is a 'must' for any serious student.

In a similar category should be placed J.J. Scarisbrick, *The Reformation and the English People* (Blackwell 1984). This has set the standard for those dealing with the topic using a 'bottom-up' approach. It is essential reading for any student studying the English Reformation 'in the round'.

The general interpretations supported by the revisionist historians are most readily accessible in C. Haig, *English Reformations* (Oxford 1993). Although most of the book is at a level of detail that would only be of relevance to those studying at degree level, something of the flavour of the revisionists' work can rapidly be acquired by dipping into one or two chapters of this book.

2 The Henrician Reformation

Those wishing to pursue the 'top-down' approach further, rather than concentrating on the 'bottom-up' approach favoured by Dickens and the revisionist historians, would find it easiest to do so via biographies of the leading characters. Both because of the central part played by the king in the Reformation during his reign and because of the very high esteem in which the book is held, the obvious starting point would be J.J. Scarisbrick, *Henry VIII* (Methuen 1968). The book's very detailed index allows the relevant sections to be selected easily. Scarisbrick's interest in the theology of the divorce led him to devote much more space to this issue than its historical significance justified but, apart from this, any reference to Henry and religion is worth following up.

Reading at least part of a biography of another character is vital if some perspective on events is to be gained. As Thomas Cranmer was involved in all aspects of the Henrician Reformation, he is probably the best person to choose, especially as a biography of him exists that also offers interesting insights into the methods used by a professional historian. To gain this, look especially at the notes and bibliography sections at the end of the book. Therefore, although it contains much more detail than you could possibly need, it would be worthwhile skim-reading a chapter or two of the massive (692 pages) D. MacCulloch, *Thomas Cranmer* (Yale 1996).

Similarly full of insights into the period (up to 1535), but with the added advantage of being brilliantly written in places, is the most highly respected of the many biographies of Thomas More. This is R. Marius, *Thomas More* (Dent 1984). The major drawback with the book is, once again, its massive length. It is therefore suggested that decisions are made about exactly which aspects of the great man's life are to be investigated before any reading is commenced.

The dissolution of the monasteries is a nicely self-contained topic and one of the many studies of the subject stands out as being especially helpful to students. The relevant text is brief and to the point (much of the book is devoted to illustrative contemporary documents) and most of the explanations are clear and concise. The book is Joyce Youings, *The Dissolution of the Monasteries* (Allen and Unwin 1971).

Index

dissolution of the smaller
    monasteries (1536) 67–8
dissolution of the larger
    monasteries (1538–40)
    68–70
why were they dissolved?
    70–6
was their dissolution pre-
    planned? 76–80
why was there so little
    opposition to their
    dissolution? 80–2
what were the effects of their
    dissolution? 82–6
More, Sir Thomas 54–7, 98,
    104, 109–10

non-residence 34, 37
Norfork, Duke of 15, 35, 127

Observant Franciscan friars
    52–3

Parr, Catherine 124
Pilgrimage of Grace (1536) 68,
    80
pluralism 34, 37
Pope – see Clement VII
    (1523–34)
praemunire 37

Reading, Abbot of 69
Reformation Parliament
    (1529–36) 35–6, 45–50
revisionist historians 96, 98, 99,
    122–3
Richmond, Duke of,
    illegitimate son of Henry
    VIII 9

Rome, Sack of (1527) 20, 22
Roper, Margaret 98

St German, Christopher 42
Scarisbrick J. J. 8, 112
Shaxton, Bishop 115
Southern Convocation 37–8
'sovereign empire' 41
Submission of the Clergy
    (1532) 40
Suffolk, Duke of 15, 35
Surrey, Earl of 126
A Supplication for the Beggars
    (1528) 93
Supplication against the
    Ordinaries (1532) 39

Ten Articles (1536) 103, 104
Tintern Abbey 82
transubstantiation 115, 116
Treasons Act (1534) 51–2
Tyndale, William 95, 104

Valor Ecclesiasticus (1535) 65–6,
    72
Visitations of 1535 66

Warham, William, Archbishop
    of Canterbury 18, 39
Westminster Abbey 83
Wiltshire, Earl of 15, 35
Wolsey, Thomas, Cardinal
    11–15
    tactics used to gain divorce
        12–14
    reasons for failure to gain
        divorce 14–15
    actions over monasteries
        64–5